ENGLISH
A MASTER FILE
KEY STAGE 2

Editors

D C Perkins, BA (Hons), MEd, PhD (Wales) and E J Perkins, BSc (Hons), MEd

Illustrations by Anthony James

These Master Files are designed for use in the classroom. Each consists of teachers' notes, pupils' resource material, worksheets, activities and record sheet. Each book covers a part of the national curriculum in depth allowing the teacher to decide the amount of material to use according to the age and ability of the children.

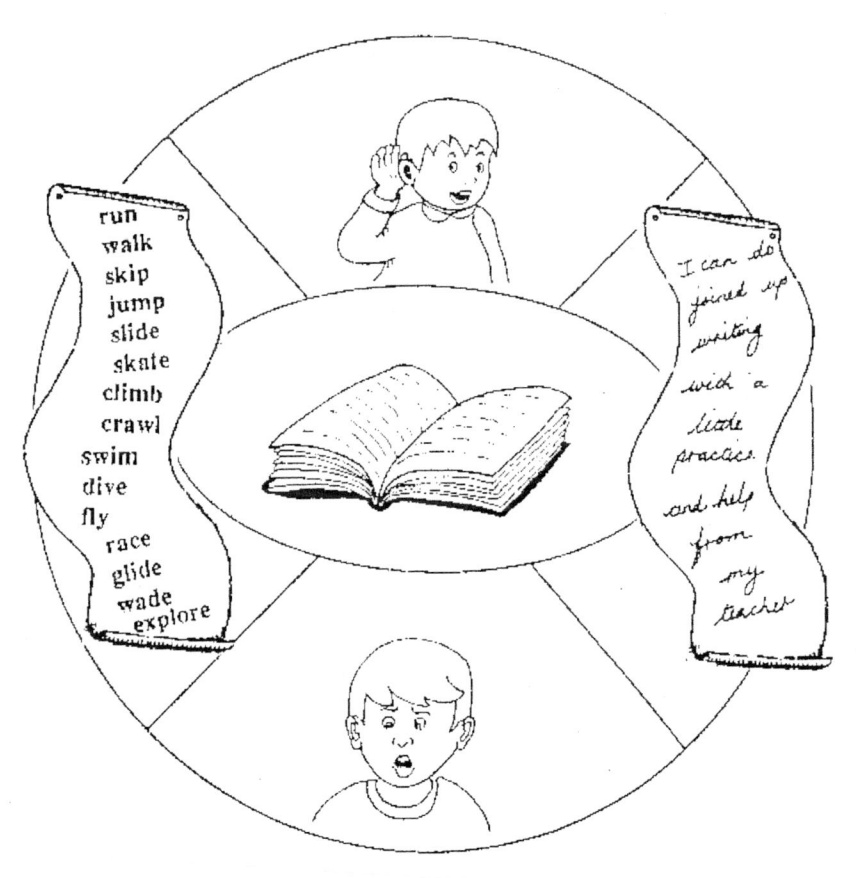

All rights reserved. This book is not copyright free. It is sold subject to the condition that it shall not, by way of trade or otherwise, be lent, hired out or otherwise circulated without the publisher's written consent. No part of this publication may be reproduced, stored in a retrieval system, or transmitted, in any form or by any means, electronic, mechanical, photocopying, recording or otherwise without the prior written permission of the publisher. All pages in this book can be photocopied for educational purposes only within the purchasing school or educational establishment. There is no limit to the number of copies that may be produced within the purchasing school or establishment and no return in respect of any photocopying licence is needed. This permission does not extend to the making of copies (e.g. in a resource centre) for use outside the institution in which they are made.

DOMINO BOOKS (WALES) LTD
SWANSEA SA1 1FN
Tel. 01792 459378 Fax. 01792 466337

English Master File KS2 © EJP & DCP 1994 ISBN 1 85772 085 7

Reprined 1995 (twice). Revised and reprinted 1996, 1997, 1998, 1999

CONTENTS 1

PUPILS' RESOURCES/WORKSHEETS

Page

SPEAKING AND LISTENING
- Speaking and Listening — 5
- Storyboard — 6
- What's Happened? — 7
- Messages — 8
- Listening — 9
- Planning a Visit — 10
- Planning a Wall Display About Where I Live — 11
- A Scientific Investigation — 12
- Be a Designer — 13
- Gardening Club — 13
- The Interview — 14
- Conservation — 15
- We Did This — 16
- Bookings — 17
- I Do Not Like Camping! — 18
- Save Our School — 19
- When My Brother (or Sister) was Born — 20
- Lost and Found — 21
- A News Programme — 22
- Who Said It? — 23

READING
- Story of the Week — 24
- Character Study — 25
- Putting a Story Together — 26
- Story Detective 1 — 27
- Story Detective 2 — 28
- Story Detective 3 — 29
- What Happens Next? — 30
- Gelert and the Wolf — 31
- Storyboard — 32
- The Front Cover of a Book — 33
- The Spine of a Book — 34
- The Contents Page of a Book — 35
- The Index of a Book — 36
- Using an Encyclopaedia — 37
- Different Voices — 38
- A Story or Poem I Have Enjoyed Reading — 39
- Travelling by Train — 40
- What Happens Next? — 41
- What Happened Before? — 42

Page

- Missing Words — 43
- The Dewey System — 44
- Where Can I Find It? — 45
- In the Kitchen — 46
- On The Farm — 47
- Finding Out — 48
- In Hospital — 49
- Bookshelf — 50
- Facts or Opinions? — 51
- Advertisements — 52
- Research Project 1 — 53
- Research Project 2 — 54
- The Right Word — 55
- The Crocodile — 56
- The Big Rock Candy Mountains — 57

WRITING
- Sentences 1 — 58
- Sentences 2 — 59
- Nouns — 60
- Doing Words 1 — 61
- Doing Words 2 — 62
- Information Sentences — 63
- Describing Words 1 — 64
- Describing Words 2 — 65
- Adverbs — 66
- Questions 1 — 67
- Questions 2 — 68
- Punctuation — 69
- Sentences 3 — 70
- Layout — 71
- Life in a Castle — 72
- The 'Royal George' — 73
- Four Things — 73
- Who Said That? — 74
- Story Cards — 75

SPELLING
- Word Families — 76
- Tenses — 77
- The Old Woman and the Physician — 78
- Prefixes and Suffixes — 79

HANDWRITING
- Handwriting — 80

Teachers' Notes and Resources Contents on next page.

CONTENTS 2

TEACHER'S NOTES AND RESOURCES

	Page		*Page*
HOW TO USE YOUR MASTER FILE	iv	A Topic Web	88
		Reading with Expression	89
TEACHERS' NOTES AND RESOURCES	81	Cataloguing Systems	89
		Scanning and Skimming	89
NATIONAL CURRICULUM		Analytical and Critical Development	89
ENGLISH LANGUAGE SKILLS KS2	82	Fact and Fiction	89
Speaking and Listening Skills	82	Use of Language	89
Reading Skills	82		
Writing Skills	82	**WRITING SKILLS**	90
Spelling Skills	82	Illustrations	90
Handwriting Skills	82	Parts of Speech	90
Presentation Skills	82	Sequencing	90
		Descriptive Work	90
SPEAKING AND LISTENING SKILLS	83	Non-chronological Writing	90
Factors in Listening, Analysing		Writing Plans	90
and Re-telling	83	People	90
Beginnings	83	Places	90
Endings	83	Revising and Redrafting	90
Main Characters	83	Layout and Punctuation	90
Location/Situation	83	Composition Material	91
Mood/Atmosphere	83	Elementary Analysis	91
Conveying Simple Messages	83	Writing for Specific Purposes	91
Listening and Commenting	84	Register	91
Following and Leading	84		
Tasks within a Group	84	**SPELLING SKILLS**	92
Further Tasks within the Classroom	84	Look, Cover, Write and Check	92
Tasks outside the Classroom	84	High Frequency Words	92
Detailed Oral Acounts	84	Checking Spelling	92
Questions and Answers	85	Prefixes	93
Working Together	86	Suffixes	94
Presentations	86		
Sustained Reporting	86	**HANDWRITING SKILLS**	95
Discussion	86		
Language For Information	86	**PRESENTATION SKILLS**	95
Group Presentations	86		
Dialect and Register	86	**MISCELLANEOUS**	
		Storyboard	96
READING SKILLS	87	Topic Web	97
Parts of a Book	87	Ideas Web	98
Reading Aloud	87	Writing A Letter	99
Silent Reading	87	Addressing an Envelope	99
Story Analysis	87	Writing Practice	100
Using the Library	87		
Topic Webs	87	Record Sheet	101
Using Contents and Indexes,			
Encyclopaedias and other Material	87		

HOW TO USE YOUR MASTER FILE

For many experienced teachers these few lines will seem superfluous. This book follows the guidelines of the National Curriculum for English Key Stage 2. The Teachers' Notes are designed to provide teaching strategies for the work. The Master File is an ideas' bank with the worksheets being used for classwork and to generate ideas. Much of the material can be used in many ways. The pictures often lend themselves to more than one exercise. For example, pictures used for scanning in the teaching of reading may also be suitable for writing exercises and discussions.

1. All the material in this book is photocopiable as defined on the first page. This means that all the material can be used in any way you wish in the classroom situation. Drawings and written material may be photocopied and adapted for further work.

2. Covering sections of the master copies with plain paper enables resource material to be used in different ways.

3. Reduction of the A4 master copies to A5 means that they can be pasted in children's exercise books. The master copies can also be enlarged to A3 making it easier for students to work on them as a group.

4. Some of the material can be used as a start for classroom projects.

5. Some of the material may be adapted and used as visual aids or *aide mémoires*. Some of the photocopies can be cut to make additional puzzles and games.

6. It may be possible to use some of the Teachers' Notes directly with more advanced and brighter children.

7. Some of the worksheets and resources are more difficult than others but we do not envisage any problems selecting the most appropriate material.

8. Some of the master copies may be used in different ways, e.g. as cloze tests, sequencing exercises and so on.

9. Project work may be done individually, in groups, or with the class as a whole.

10. Use the worksheets as an ideas' bank and devise your own material.

We hope you find the book useful and welcome any comments.

Name

SPEAKING AND LISTENING

1. Close your eyes and listen carefully. Say what you can hear.
   What do you think is happening outside the classroom, in the corridor, in the school grounds, above in the sky?

2. Say what you would hear if your school were near
   an airport,   a railway,
   a bus station,   a fire station,
   a police station,   a hospital,
   a leisure centre,   building works.

3. Say what you would hear if your school were
   in the country,   near the centre of a city.

4. Can you tell whether it is night time or day time with your eyes closed?
   Give reasons for your answer.

5. With your eyes closed, listen to another pupil talking. Can you tell who it is?

6. With your eyes closed, listen to another pupil imitating someone else.
   Can you tell who is talking and who he or she is pretending to be?

7. Tell a story beginning:
   The beam from my gaoler's torch lit up glowing green slime oozing between the grey stones of the narrow, winding tunnel. He unlocked the door with the huge key hanging from his belt and pushed me into the dungeon. There was no window, no chink of light. My head struck the floor as my tormentor turned the key, locking me in. I lay still, holding my breath, listening. The darkness was full of little noises. I was not alone . . .

8. Tell a story (true or untrue) entitled 'The Amazing Adventure of . . .'

Name _____

STORYBOARD

A good storyteller knows that a story should have a BEGINNING, a MIDDLE and an END. You may remember the ending of a story first and then remember how it began. It is helpful to use a storyboard. Ideas and points can be written on the storyboard and then you can decide in which order you will tell the story. It is always helpful to give your story a title although this may be changed later. A title which is changed in this way is called a 'working title'. Some suggestions are given on this storyboard. It sometimes helps to say in one sentence what the story is about. Add drawings or photographs if you have them.

TITLE _____

This story is about _____

_____

Most important character (s)	How the story starts, the beginning.

Describe where the story takes place.

Set the mood of the story.

What happens next, the middle of the story.	How the story ends.

English KS2 Master File © E J P & D C P   Speaking and Listening/A Storyboard

WHAT'S HAPPENED?

Look at these pictures. What will the character/s in each picture say when he or she telephones for help (or contacts mission control)?

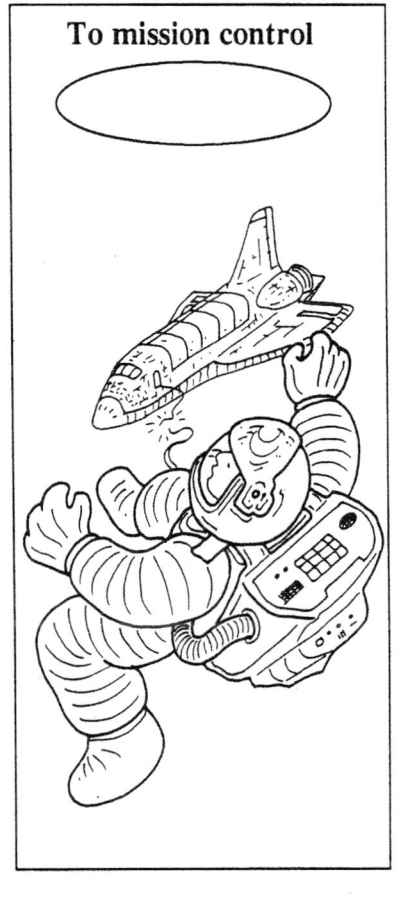

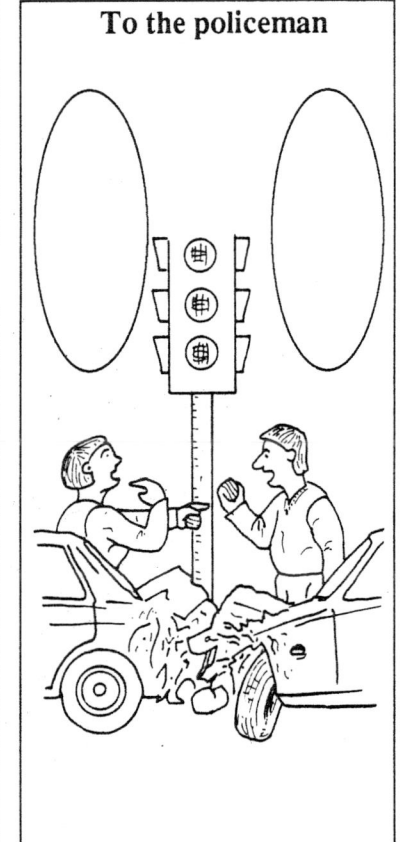

To the car mechanic	To the fireman	To mission control

To the optician	To the dentist	

To the policeman

To the barber	To the plumber	

English KS2 Master File © E J P & D C P   Speaking and Listening/What's Happened? 7

Name _____

MESSAGES

1. Your mother sends you to tell your sister or brother to take the dog for a walk.
   What do you say to your sister or brother?

   Bob

2. Your sister's friend, Bob, telephones to say that he will be late.
   What will you tell your sister?
   (You have a special nickname for Bob, you call him Stick Insect!)

3. Your headteacher,
   M _____ ,
   asks you to tell your teacher,
   M _____ ,
   that the governors' meeting has finished and the library is now open for your class to use.

   What will you say to your teacher?

4. These two workmen are having problems with the building plans they are supposed to follow. Jim (the one with the shovel) thinks the plans are wrong and George, his friend, thinks they have been given the wrong plans. Jim tells George to ring the chief engineer, Mr McMasters, and explain their problems.
   What does George say to Mr McMasters?

   What do you think Mr McMasters says?
   What does George say to Jim?

5. What difficult telephone messages have you had to pass on to someone?
   What did you say?

English KS2 Master File © E J P & D C P   Speaking and Listening/Messages 8

Name _____

LISTENING

1. Listen to a radio programme. When it has finished, say what it was about.
   If it was a play or story, tell the story.
   If it was a discussion, what were the main points? Do you agree with what was said? Give reasons for your answer.
   Does everybody listening to a recording give the same answers?
   Why may the answers be different?

2. Listen to the middle part of a tape recording of a radio programme.
   Say what you think the programme is about.
   How do you think the programme started?
   Say how you think the programme will end.
   Give reasons for your answers.
   Listen to the recording of the whole programme to find out if you were right.

3. Watch a video recording of a television programme with the sound turned down so that you cannot hear what is being said.
   Say what you think the people on the television are saying.
   Listen to the recording with normal sound to find out if you were right.

4. Listen to a video recording of a television progamme with your eyes shut so that you cannot see the screen.
   Say what you think the people on the television are doing.
   Watch the recording to find out if you were right.
   Does everybody watching the recording have the same answers?
   Why may the answers be different?

5. Watch the middle part of a video recording of a television programme.
   Say what you think happened at the beginning of the programme.
   Say how you think the programme ends.
   Give reasons for your answers.
   Does everybody watching the recording have the same answers?
   Why may the answers be different?

6. Record an episode of a 'soap' like 'Grange Hill' or 'Neighbours'.
   Say how the programme tells you what has happened in previous episodes.
   How does it make you want to watch the next episode?

English KS2 Master File © E J P & D C P   Speaking and Listening/Listening 9

Name _____

PLANNING A VISIT

We are going to _____

on (day) _____ (date) _____ at (time) _____

We shall be back _____

What we are going to do _____

_____

_____

How we are getting there _____

_____

Cost including spending money _____

_____

Kind of weather we may expect _____

_____

Things we need to take with us including any special equipment

_____

_____

_____

Food we need to take with us _____

_____

Clothes we need to wear _____

Clothes we need to pack (for travel, activities, fun and for the weather)

_____

_____

Special notes

_____

Name _____

PLANNING A WALL DISPLAY ABOUT WHERE I LIVE

How big is the wall space for the display?

Who is going to see it? (Is it for adults or children or both?)

I will find a lot of the information I need at the local library. (The class may visit the library together.)

Do I live in a village, a country town, a capital city, a tourist centre, an industrial area, a port . . .?

Make several headings such as

What was important in the past   What is important today
Local industry   Recreation   What is special about the area

I will probably change or add to these headings later.

I need to talk to people about the history of the area where I live especially about important events that have happened in the past. I should talk to people who have lived in the area for a long time beginning with my parents then other relatives, friends and neighbours.

Have any famous people been born or lived in my area?

I need to know about the geography of the area and what is special about the location. Is it near the sea or a river or mountains . . . ?

I need to know what is important about the area today.

I need to collect photographs, pictures and maps or take photograhs and make drawings of the area and events.

Does the area have any special problems?

Things I like and dislike about where I live.

Make a plan on paper to show how the display is to be arranged before putting it on the wall.

Remember to take care of any photographs or anything else you are loaned and return them when the display is taken down.

A SCIENTIFIC INVESTIGATION

1. Give an account of how you found the volume of a bottle.
[Begin with a list of the equipment you used: bowl, measuring jug and the bottle.
Steps in the experiment.
Half fill the bowl with water.
Completely fill the bottle with water.
Pour the water from the bottle into the measuring jug. (Be careful not to spill any water.)
Read the volume of water in the measuring jug.
The volume of water in the jug is equal to the volume of the bottle.
Be careful to state the units correctly.]

2. Give an account of how you investigated the kinds of things which float in water.
[Steps in the experiment.
Half fill a bowl with water.
Gently place pieces of different substances on the surface. Do they float or sink?
The results are put in two columns headed

       Floats   Sinks

Substances/objects used: piece of wood, a cork, a coin, a piece of plastic, a lead ball, a tennis ball, an ice cube, sand, a balloon full of air, a candle, a glass marble, an empty bottle . . .]

Ships are mainly made from metal but they float. Why do they float?
What is the Plimsoll line?

Name _____

BE A DESIGNER
GARDENING CLUB

1. **Design a Birthday Card**
   Tell the class or a group of pupils how to make a birthday card.

   Discuss the size and shape of the card and what it should be made of.
   What is the age of the person for whom the card is intended?
   Discuss what should be put on the outside of the card. What does this depend on?
   What should be put inside the card? Is it to have a verse?
   Let the children make different cards in class or at home and make a wall display from them.

2. **Gardening Club**
   Tell the class or a group of pupils how to make a wild flower garden.

   Discuss why this is a good thing to do. [Natural habitats like woods, commons and hedges are being destroyed; the spraying of crops and grass verges with insecticides, herbicides and other chemicals kills wild flowers; in gardens they are often treated as weeds and destroyed.
   Wild flowers are beautiful and are important for many insects such as butterflies. Some may also become important in medicine in the future. You may be able to think of lots more reasons to make a wild flower garden.]
   Discuss where the garden can be made: a corner in the school garden or the garden at home may be left alone so that wild flowers can grow there - the wind and birds will drop the seeds on to the patch of soil or a box of earth left in the open.
   This project will take a long time. Discuss how its progress can be measured.
   Discuss how often the garden should be inspected, perhaps once a week in the summer and less often in the winter.
   Discuss what the pupils should look for - plants, insects, birds. Make drawings and take photographs. Always make a note of the date and time the gardens are visited.
   Discuss how the results of all the class or group can be recorded and compared.

Name _____

THE INTERVIEW

1. Listen to the tapes of several interviews from the radio or television.

   Discuss the following.

   What kind of people are interviewed?
   Why are people interviewed?
   When are people interviewed?
   Where are people interviewed?
   Who does the interviewing?

   Do you think interviews are good or bad? Are they interesting? Are they important?
   Do you always believe the answers people give when they are questioned?
   Are interviews always 'fair'?
   What kind of interviews do you find most interesting?
   Give reasons for your answers.

2. Name a person you would like to interview and explain your choice.
   What questions would you like to ask?

   Practise the interview. A friend or another pupil can pretend to be the person you have chosen and you can ask the questions. Change places.

3. Suppose you are the manager of a shop and you want to employ an assistant.
   What kind of person would you need?
   You decide to interview someone for the job. Discuss the questions you would ask him or her at the interview.
   What would you say about the job?
   How would you decide if the person is suitable? Would this depend on his or her answers only?

   Suppose you apply for the job of shop assistant.
   Why would you like the job?
   What questions would you ask at the interview?
   What would you wear?
   What would make you decide to take the job (or refuse it) if it was offered?

4. Imaginary interview
   Suppose you meet an alien from outer space (who has a decoder so that he can understand you and speak to you).
   What questions would you ask him?
   What questions do you think he would ask you?

5. Talk to the Animals
   Suppose your pet could speak.
   What questions would you ask it?
   What questions do you think it would ask you?

Name _____

CONSERVATION

Plan an article for the school magazine or a local paper on conservation in your area. Begin with a 'working title' and decide how many words should be in the article. Discuss conservation in your area and use this storyboard to help you organise the contents of the article.

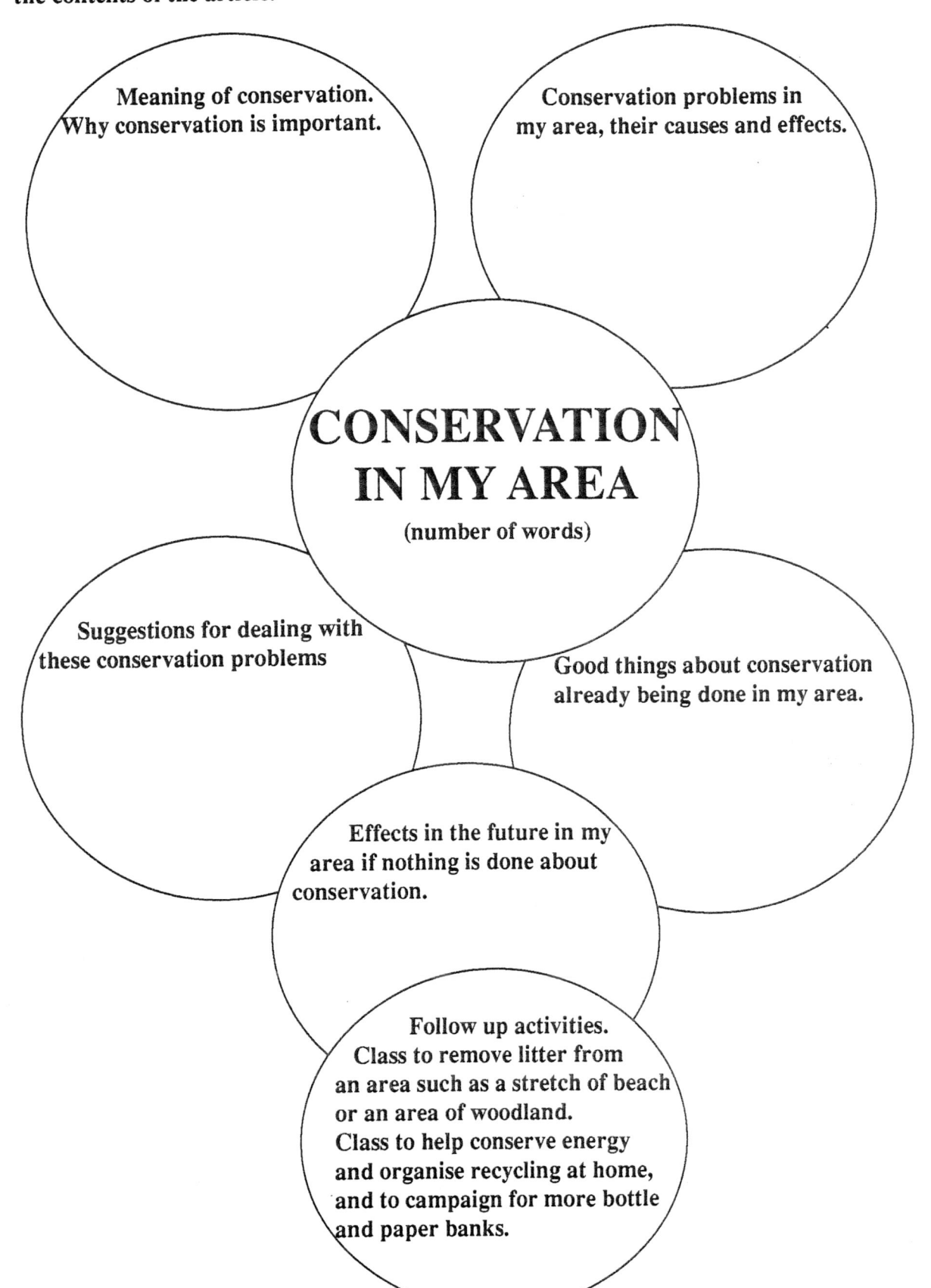

- Meaning of conservation. Why conservation is important.
- Conservation problems in my area, their causes and effects.

CONSERVATION IN MY AREA
(number of words)

- Suggestions for dealing with these conservation problems
- Good things about conservation already being done in my area.
- Effects in the future in my area if nothing is done about conservation.
- Follow up activities. Class to remove litter from an area such as a stretch of beach or an area of woodland. Class to help conserve energy and organise recycling at home, and to campaign for more bottle and paper banks.

Name _____

WE DID THIS

Discuss an activity or event in which a group or the whole class took part.
Give an account of what was done, when and where.
Who organised it?
Why was it organised?
Who took part?
What were the results? Was it a success?
Would you like to take part in something similar again? (Give reasons for your answer.)
Are there any ways in which it could be improved?
Are there any other activities or events you would like to take part in?

Name _____

BOOKINGS

1. You telephone a guest house to book a room for two nights. What do you say?

2. You and your classmate have booked two rooms at a guest house for a short holiday.
   Another classmate pretends to be the landlady of the guest house.
   The landlady greets you when you arrive.
   [Continue the conversation until you are shown your rooms and the landlady leaves.
   You confirm details such as your names, addressess, when you will be leaving and
   how you will pay the accounts.]

3. As in 2, you and your classmate pretend to be the guests at a guest house.
   The landlady greets you when you arrive but she cannot find your booking.
   [Continue the conversation. There are only two small rooms (attics really) available.
   All the other rooms are full.]

4. You have booked a special-rate weekend at a luxury hotel in the country for yourself
   and your family. The hotel has written to you confirming your booking.
   Say what happens from the time you arrive until you are shown your rooms.
   [Other pupils play the parts of the family, hotel manager, receptionist, porter and
   other guests in the reception area.]

5. Give an account of any problems you have experienced on holiday. What happened
   in the end?

English KS2 Master File © E J P & D C P   Speaking and Listening/Bookings 17

Name _____

I DO NOT LIKE CAMPING!

You have allowed yourself to be persuaded to join friends for a weekend camping holiday and this is a sketch of you inside the tent.
Give an account of what happened.

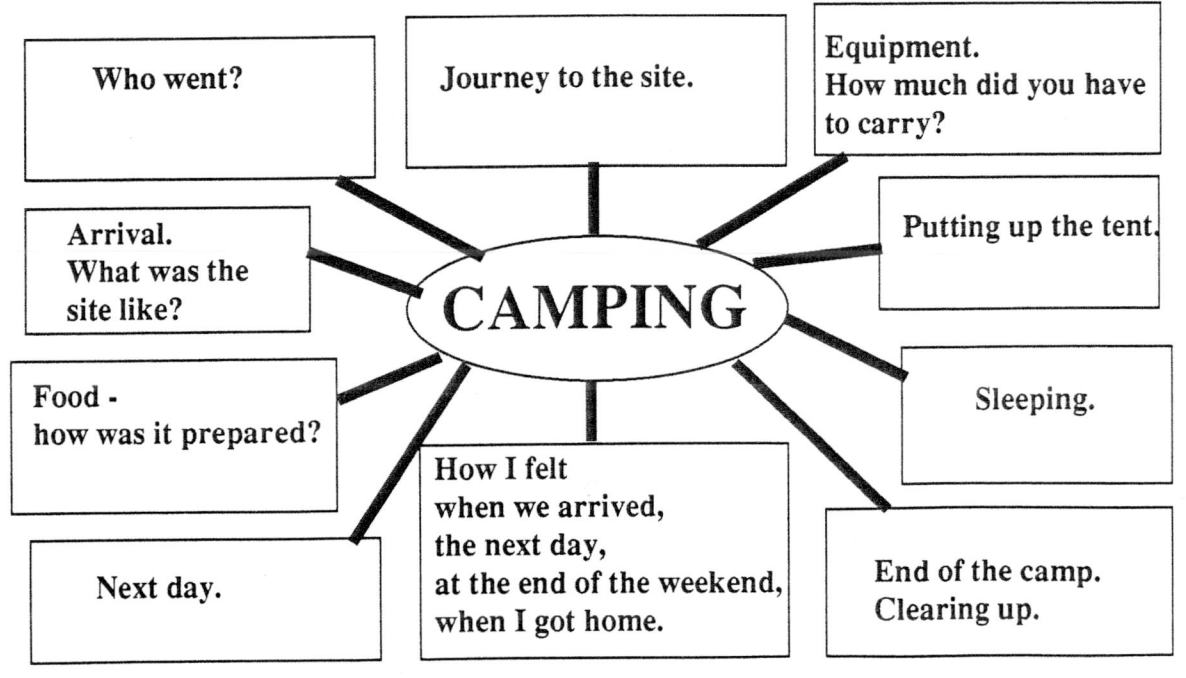

- Who went?
- Journey to the site.
- Equipment. How much did you have to carry?
- Putting up the tent.
- Arrival. What was the site like?
- Sleeping.
- Food - how was it prepared?
- How I felt when we arrived, the next day, at the end of the weekend, when I got home.
- Next day.
- End of the camp. Clearing up.

CAMPING

English KS2 Master File © E J P & D C P

Speaking and Listening/I Do Not Like Camping! 18

Name _____

S O S
SAVE OUR SCHOOL

Suppose you have been told that your 'old' school is going to close at the end of the next term. You have been asked to speak at a meeting in the school hall organised by parents who do not want the school to close.

Your speech might include the following

Why you like the school.

What the school is like - how good it is.
Good examination results.
It trains people for local work.

When it was founded and its traditions.

Its importance to the people who live near it and who send their children to it.
Its role in the community.
Our parents went there and it is seen as a focal point for local functions.

Disadvantages of closing the school.
Children would have to travel further to another school. They would have to travel in the dark in the winter.

People with children may move away to be closer to the new school.
If this happened the area would have a smaller and 'ageing' population and local shops might have to close.

Staff have been at the school for a long time and work well as a team.

The School Hall is used for local meetings.

The school uses the local leisure centre which would miss the fees paid by the school.

The school has a very good band and choir which would be broken up.

Notes for your speech

Name _____

WHEN MY BROTHER (OR SISTER) WAS BORN

The arrival of a new baby can mean lots of changes in the family. Explain how you felt about the arrival of your baby brother or sister.

- Looking forward to the new baby.
  Will things be the same?
  I feel

- Mum is the centre of attention.
  Dad is worried about her.
  I try to help but
  I feel

- Mum is tired sometimes and does not do as much for me as she used to.
  I try to understand and help her but sometimes
  I feel

MY FEELINGS

- Dad takes Mum to the hospital. I am not allowed to go and I feel

  I stay with an aunt.

- Mum takes me shopping to buy clothes for the new baby. I get some new clothes too which I did not expect.
  I think

  I hug Mum.

- Visit Mum at the hospital.
  I am allowed to hold the baby.
  He/she is great and
  I feel

- I help Dad to finish the baby's room.
  Dad says I must help look after the new baby and
  I feel

Name _____

LOST...

MY PET

Explain how you lost your pet and draw a picture of it.
Say what your pet is like and show a photograph or drawing of it.
Does it have a name tag with a contact telephone number on it?
Describe your pet, say what it likes and dislikes and what frightens it.
Say what you think it will do.
Has it happened before? Some pets run away to wherever they have lived before.
Explain how you are trying to find it.

If you decide to put an advertisement in the Lost and Found column of the local newspaper or a notice/card in the window of the local newsagent, what will you write?

AND FOUND

You have found a wallet.
Explain how and where you found it.
Describe the wallet and say what is inside it.
Explain what you have done with it.

WHAT IS IT?

Close your eyes and have someone give you a small object. With your eyes still closed, examine the object with your hands and say what it is.

What cannot be discovered about an object by touch alone?

With your eyes closed, try to identify a person by touch alone.

What kinds of things cannot be discovered about a person by touch alone?

Name _____

A NEWS PROGRAMME

Plan a news programme.
Decide who is going to collect the news, who is going to write it, who is going to present it and who is to be the programme controller or anchor person. The way in which each item is treated, depends on what it is about.

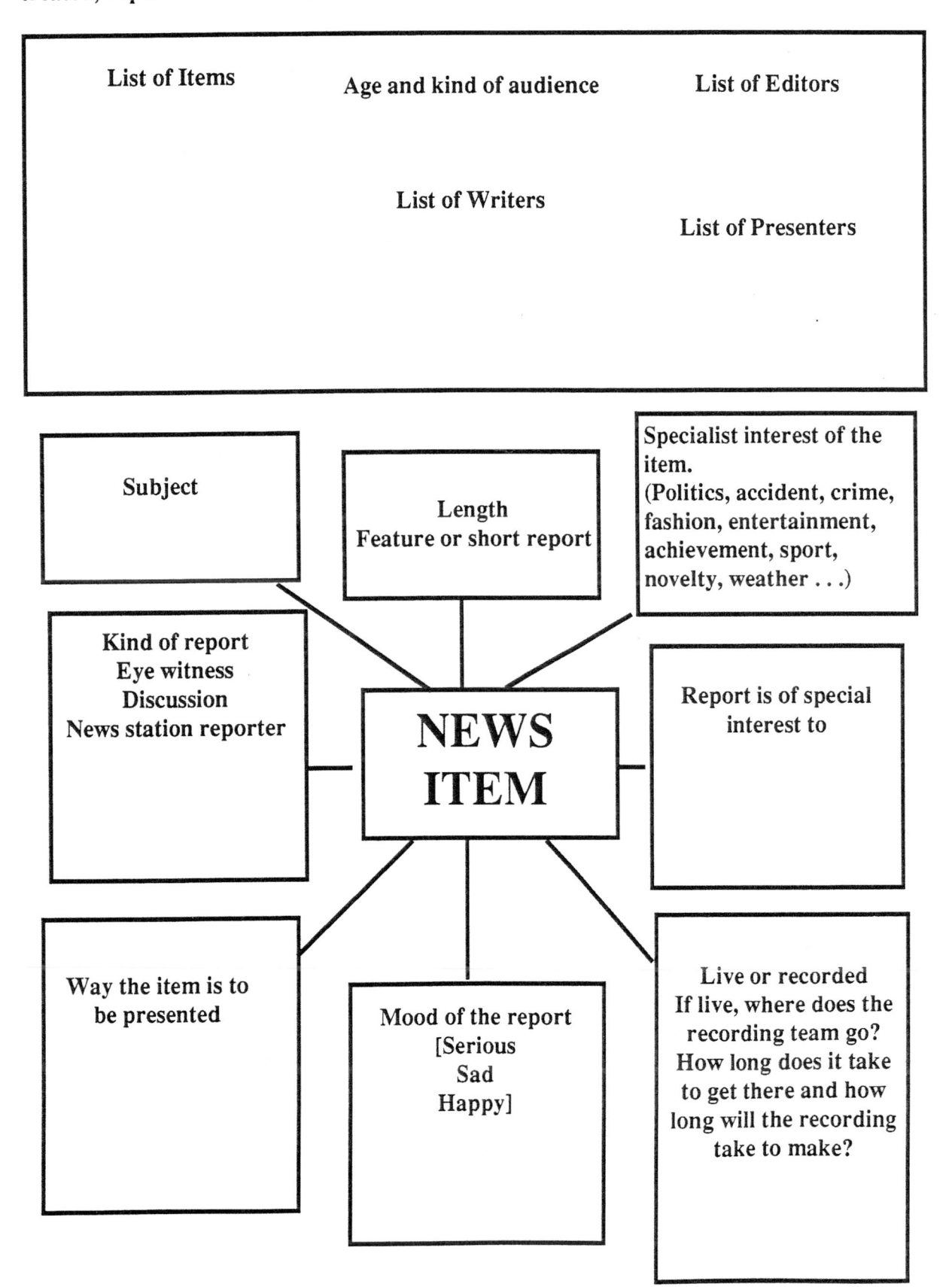

List of Items   Age and kind of audience   List of Editors

       List of Writers

                                                     List of Presenters

---

Subject

Length — Feature or short report

Specialist interest of the item. (Politics, accident, crime, fashion, entertainment, achievement, sport, novelty, weather ...)

Kind of report — Eye witness / Discussion / News station reporter

NEWS ITEM

Report is of special interest to

Way the item is to be presented

Mood of the report [Serious / Sad / Happy]

Live or recorded — If live, where does the recording team go? How long does it take to get there and how long will the recording take to make?

English KS2 Master File © E J P & D C P   Speaking and Listening/A News Programme 22

Name _____

WHO SAID IT?

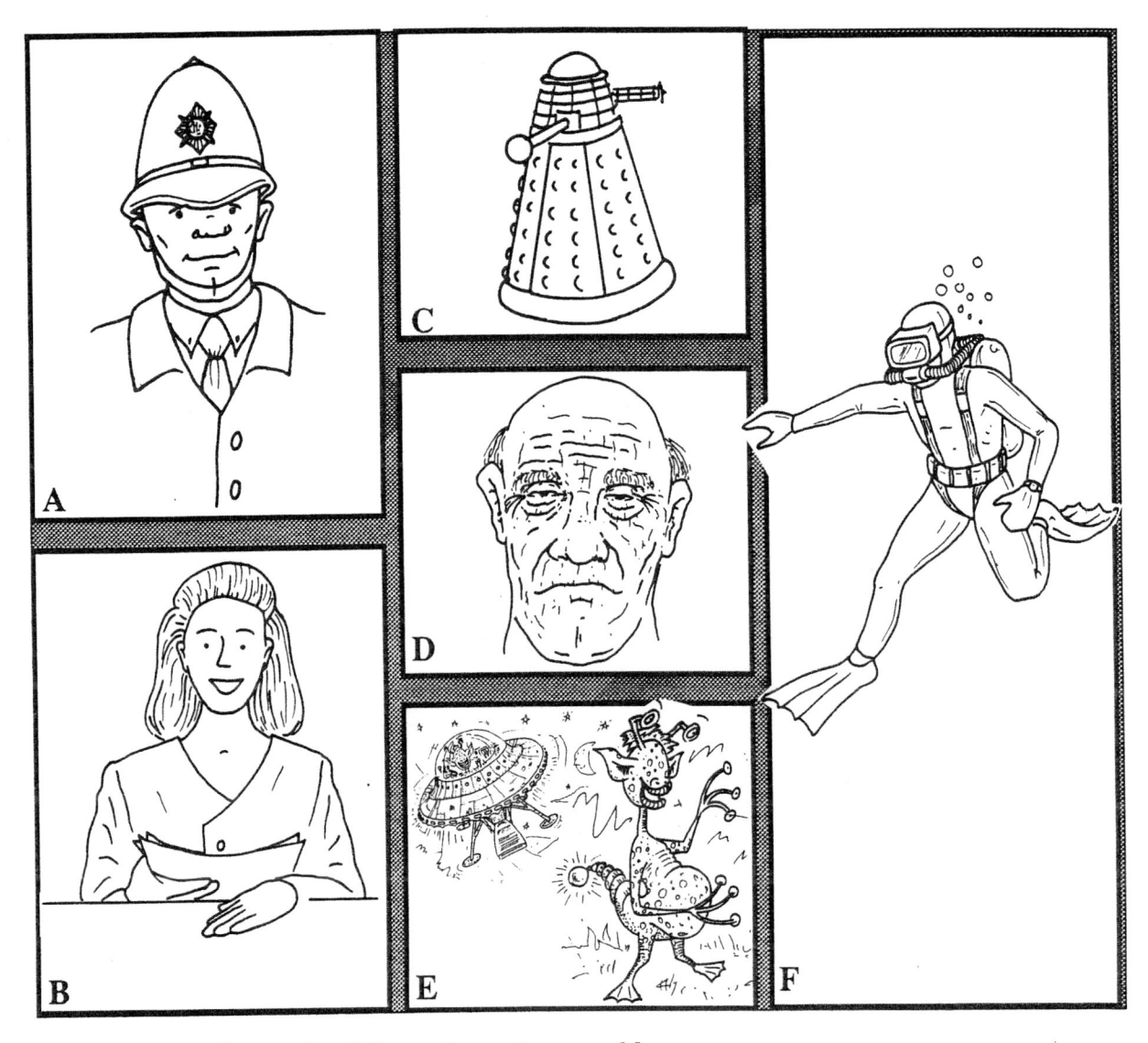

How do you think each of these characters would say

'Who broke the window? I want a straight answer to a straight question. Do you understand me?'

Would they all use the same words?

Say if the characters are likely to be sad, frightened, cross or happy.

Who do you think would say the following?

1. 'Excuse me, sir, can I help you?
2. 'This is the 6 o'clock news.'
3. 'Can I come up now?'
4. 'Exterminate, exterminate...'
5. 'Where am I?'
6. 'My name is 'arry and I don't want no trouble.'

Make up a short story or play about some or all of these characters.

English KS2 Master File © E J P & D C P   Speaking and Listening/Who Said It? 23

Name _____

STORY OF THE WEEK

Read aloud all or part of your favourite story.

Pretend to be each character as you read.

Which is your favourite character?

Keep a record of the stories you read.

Title
Author
Characters
Where and when the story is set
What the story is about
How the story starts
How the story continues - what happens next
How the story ends
Is there anything special about the story?
I like/dislike the story because

Name _____

CHARACTER STUDY

My favourite character is

He/she/it is in

I like this character because

Another character I like is

He/she/it is in

I like this character because

These characters are alike/different because

The character I dislike most is

He/she/it is in

I do not like this character because

Write a story or poem about one of these characters.

Name _____

PUTTING A STORY TOGETHER

Imagine that putting a story together is like climbing a mountain.

A story has three parts, a BEGINNING, a MIDDLE and the END. These are sometimes broken up into smaller sections. The parts are held together by the storyline or the plot. Using the storyboard below means you can work on any part at any time. You may prefer to use a different sheet of paper to work out each part or use index cards.

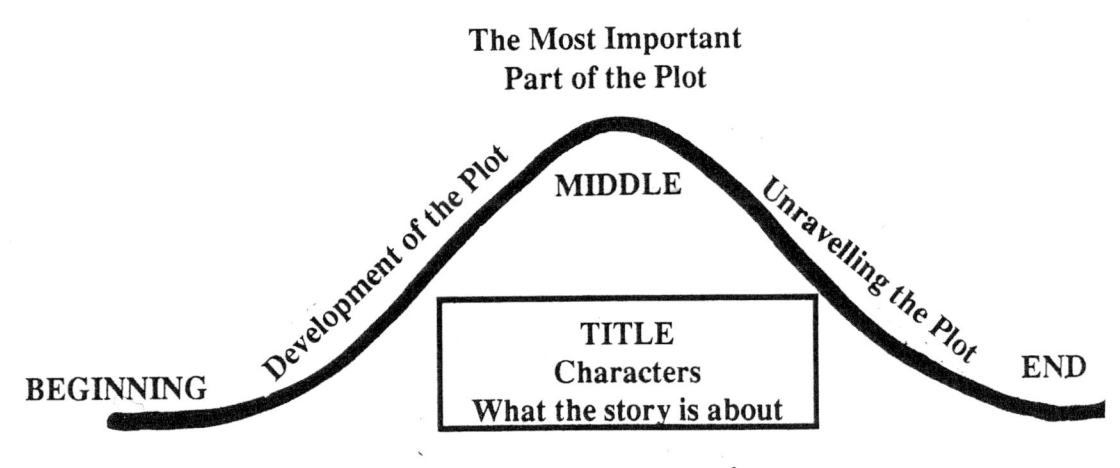

```
            The Most Important
             Part of the Plot
                    
         Development    MIDDLE    Unravelling
         of the Plot              the Plot
                    ┌─────────────┐
                    │    TITLE    │
                    │  Characters │
BEGINNING           │What the story│           END
                    │   is about  │
                    └─────────────┘
```

1. Give your story a title. By	
2. Decide what the story is about.	6. Decide how the story begins.
	7. Decide how the story continues - what happens next.
3. Decide the characters - who they are and who are the most important. Write a little about each - what they are like, what they look like, how they talk ...	8. Decide what is the most important event or action.
	9. Solve any problems in the plot.
4. Decide where and when the story takes place.	10. THE ENDING
5. Decide the mood/atmosphere of the story.	

English KS2 Master File © E J P & D C P   Reading/Putting a Story Together 26

Name

STORY DETECTIVE 1

These pictures come from two stories. In each case draw the missing middle picture then give the story a title and write the middle part.

TITLE _____   TITLE _____

Name _____

STORY DETECTIVE 2

These two pictures are part of a story. Draw the missing middle picture then give the story a title and write the whole story.

Title

By

English KS2 Master File © E J P & D C P   Reading/Story Detective 2   28

Name _____

STORY DETECTIVE 3

These two pictures are part of a story. Draw the missing middle picture then give the story a title and write the whole story.

Title

By

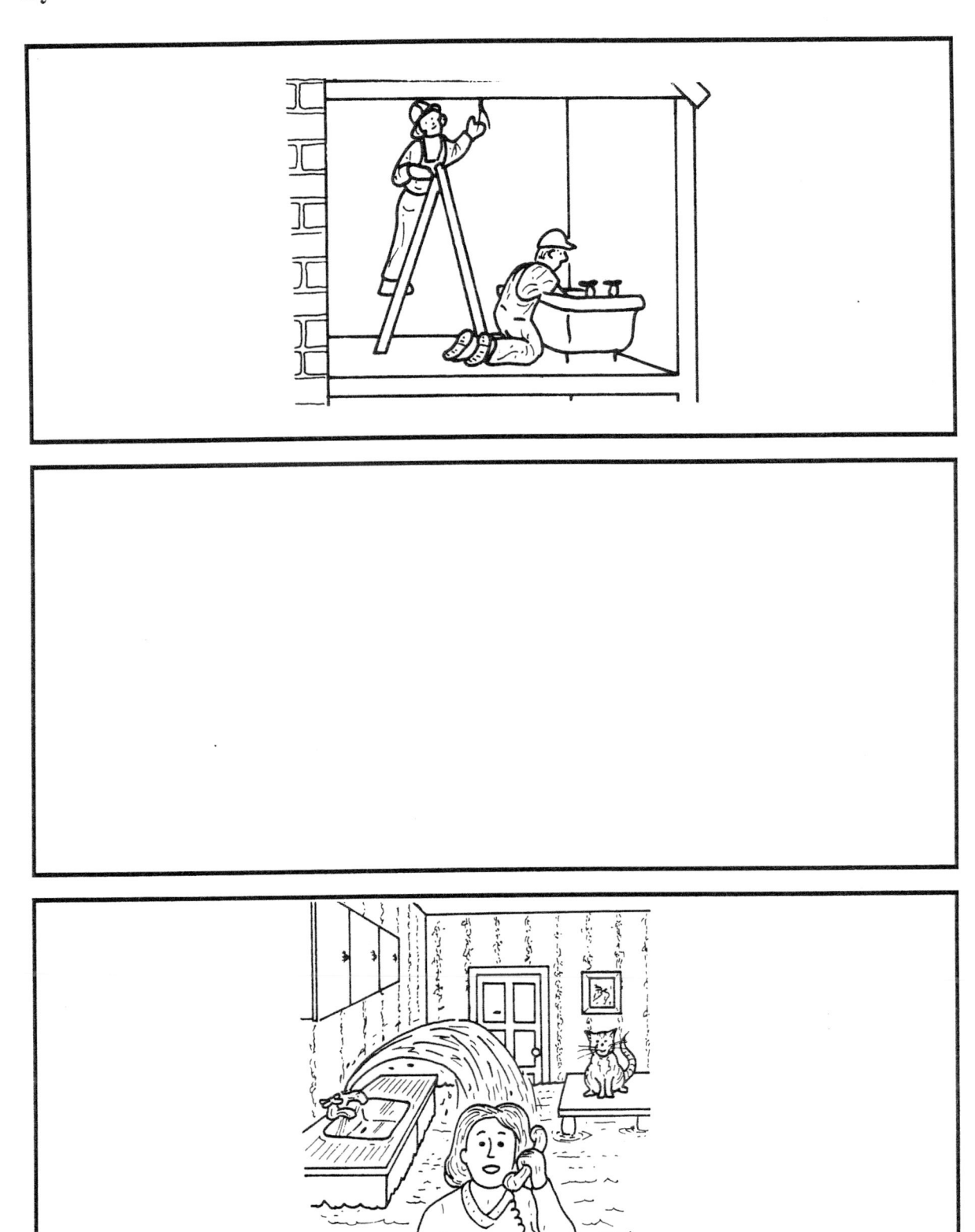

Name _____

WHAT HAPPENS NEXT?

Complete the story and draw a picture to illustrate it.

Joey was a born collector. Keeping Joey's room tidy was a full time job and his mother threatened that anything left in the wrong place would be thrown out. He kept his most precious treasures out of sight in a large box under his bed. When it was raining and he could not go out, he sorted the box, lovingly holding each item in the palms of his hands. There was the cricket ball, warm with summer sun, that had given him the winning catch last term. There was the victorious, vinegar hardened conker that seemed to be growing a mould. Carefully he dusted it with the duvet cover before putting it back in the box. Then there was the big stone. He had found it on the edge of the cliff at the back of the house. He liked the colour, grey, blue and pink at the same time, and the feel of it in his hands. Once or twice he thought it had moved slightly. Perhaps it was magic. His mother wanted to use it as a door stop but he had rescued it.

'Joey, I hope you are working and not wasting your time with all that rubbish.'

Joey heard his mother climbing the stairs and quickly pushed his box out of sight under the bed against the radiator.

A few nights later, Joey heard a small cracking noise beneath him . . .

_____

_____

Name

_____

_____

_____

_____

_____

_____

English KS2 Master File © E J P & D C P   Reading/What Happens Next?

Name _____

GELERT AND THE WOLF

Complete this story in two ways with two different endings.

When the little prince was born, Gelert decided that it should be his special responsibility to look after the baby. There had been rumours that a wolf had been seen near the hunting lodge but the Prince shrugged his shoulders and told the Princess that Gelert would soon see off any predator who came near the lodge and ensure that no harm came to their baby.

'Gelert was given to me as a tiny puppy and I trust him completely,' the Prince said.

One morning, the lodge was strangely quiet. The servants, usually laughing and chattering were silent and one maid seemed to have been crying. Someone or something had left muddy paw marks all over the floor. As well the bones and meat from the previous day were missing.

Gelert sniffed the marks and growled deep within his throat, recognising the scent. The wolf had been inside the lodge. Gelert barked, trying to make everyone understand the danger but no one listened to him . . .

First Ending	Second Ending

Name _____

STORYBOARD

Use this storyboard to write your own story.

TITLE	
By	
The story is about.	The story continues - what happens next (the middle)
Characters	
	The most important event or action
Where the story takes place (location)	
	Problems in the plot to be worked out
When the story takes place	
	Working towards the ending
Mood/atmosphere	
The story begins (the beginning)	The ending

Name _____

THE FRONT COVER OF A BOOK

THE STORY OF THE VIKINGS

by

John Reilly Jones

Illustrations by René Davidson

Study the cover of the book above and then answer these questions.

1. What is the title of the book?

2. What is the book about?

3. Who is the author of the book?

4. Who did the drawings for the book?

Name _____

THE SPINE OF A BOOK

BIRDS

LOUISA PIPPS

DOMINO

This is the spine of a book.

The title of the book is _____

The author is _____

The publisher is _____

Is the publisher the same as the printer? _____

Write the title of the book most likely to contain the answers or information for the following.

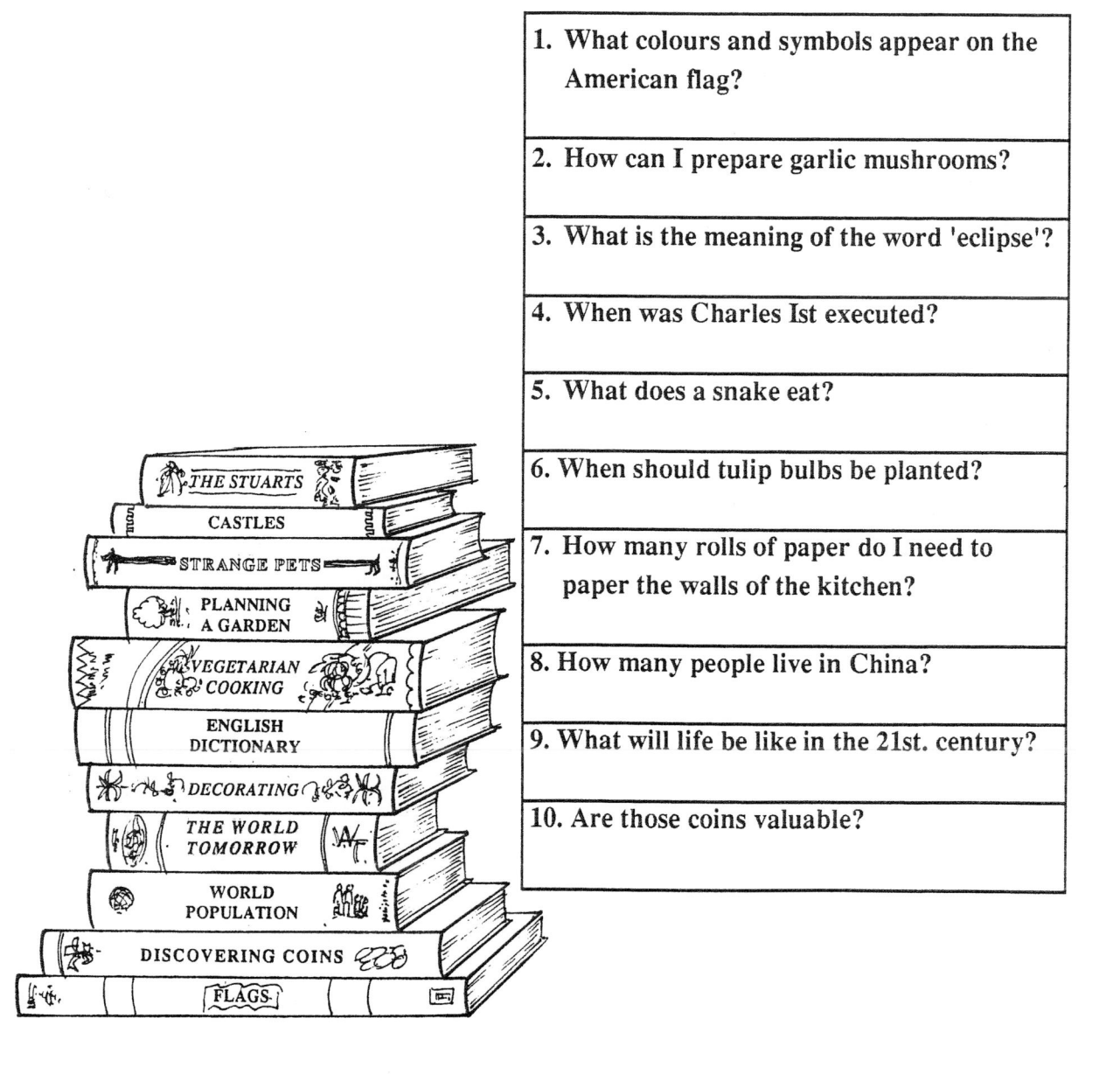

1. What colours and symbols appear on the American flag?
2. How can I prepare garlic mushrooms?
3. What is the meaning of the word 'eclipse'?
4. When was Charles Ist executed?
5. What does a snake eat?
6. When should tulip bulbs be planted?
7. How many rolls of paper do I need to paper the walls of the kitchen?
8. How many people live in China?
9. What will life be like in the 21st. century?
10. Are those coins valuable?

Books in stack:
- THE STUARTS
- CASTLES
- STRANGE PETS
- PLANNING A GARDEN
- VEGETARIAN COOKING
- ENGLISH DICTIONARY
- DECORATING
- THE WORLD TOMORROW
- WORLD POPULATION
- DISCOVERING COINS
- FLAGS

English KS2 Master File © E J P & D C P   Reading/The Spine of a Book 34

Name _____

THE CONTENTS PAGE OF A BOOK

This is the contents page from the book, 'Monsters from the Past'.

CONTENTS

		Page
	Introduction	5
Chapter 1	How Fossils are Formed	10
Chapter II	The Food of Dinosaurs	15
Chapter III	Dinosaur Dimensions	20
Chapter IV	Record Breakers	28
Chapter V	Animals of the Dinosaur World	34
Chapter VI	Dinosaurs - Fact and Fiction	39
	Index	50

DIMETRODON

In which chapters would you find the following information?
The first has been done for you.

1. What did dinosaurs eat?

   Chapter II The Food of Dinosaurs, page 15.

2. What evidence is there that dinosaurs really existed?

3. How big were dinosaurs?

4. What made dinosaurs unusual?

5. What creatures lived at the same time as the dinosaurs?

6. Where would you find an alphabetical list of everything in the book?

STYRACOSAURUS

TRICERATOPS

STEGOSAURUS

DIPLODOCUS

PROTOCERATOPS

TYRANNOSAURUS

POLACANTHUS

English KS2 Master File © E J P & D C P

Name _____

THE INDEX OF A BOOK

This is part of the index of a book about things to do on holiday.

INDEX

Acting in plays, 3	Games, 7
Beach games, 8	Gardening, 27
Brightening up old clothes, 13	Holiday newspaper, 28
	Indoor games, 9
Camping, 15	Jewellery, 21
Card games, 9	Outdoor games, 11
Cards, 9	Painting, 31
Clay jewellery, 22	Paper flowers, 24
Clay modelling, 23	Parties, 32
Collecting things, 25	Photography, 30
Cooking, 18	Picnics, 20
Fancy dress, 5	Puppets, 4
Food, 17	Swimming, 26

On which pages are the following subjects found in the book?

Subject	Page Number	Subject	Page Number
How to put on a play		How to take better photographs	
How to have a healthy diet		Beach ball games	
Meals outdoors		Collecting shells	
How to be a better swimmer		Organising a Spelling Bee	
How to make a party cake		Tie and dye a scarf	
Planning a holiday newspaper		Clock patience	
How to brighten up a T-shirt		Making a sock puppet	
Ways of starting a garden		Gingerbread	
What to take camping		Cards	
Party drinks		Paper roses	
How to make a badge from clay		Dressing up	

Write out the contents page of the book.

English KS2 Master File © E J P & D C P

USING AN ENCYCLOPAEDIA

Volumes:
- A B C — 1
- D E F — 2
- G H I — 3
- J K L — 4
- M N O — 5
- P Q R — 6
- S T U — 7
- V W X Y Z — 8
- INDEX — 9

In which volumes of the encyclopaedia would you find information on the following topics?

The first one has been done for you.

Subject	Volume	Subject	Volume	Subject	Volume
Animals	1	Metals		The Romans	
Bees		Wood		Birthdays	
Spiders		Fashion		Tea	
The Yeti		Glaciers		Telephones	
Deserts		Yams		Space Travel	
Photography		Automobiles		Printing	
Zoos		China		Cinema	
Chocolate		Knots		Sugar	
Religious Festivals		Ivory		Agriculture	
Aeroplanes		Christmas		London	
Dinosaurs		William Shakespeare		Computers	
				Alphabetical list of subjects in the encyclopaedia	

Name _____

DIFFERENT VOICES

Read these pieces aloud and pretend you are the character speaking.

My name is Trojan and I have come to earth to exterminate my enemies. With my powerful computer, I can control all you earthlings. You cannot resist me, it is useless to try.

Water! Water! Is that water?

Keep away from me. I warn you. I must not get wet. My workable parts will rust and I shall not be able to move.

I heard that. I will not make good scrap metal. I will not make any sort of scrap metal. I shall destroy you all.

My name is Purslane and I am a weed. My life is miserable. No one admires my beauty and no one likes me.

Once there were thousands of us in this field. Now we are reduced to a scattering amongst the crops the farmer has planted.

The farmer sprays me to try and kill me. So far he has not succeeded. He killed my mother and father last year but I survived as a seed in the soil until it was warmer and the rain fell. Others of my family survived in the hedgerows.

The music goes round and round,

Get with it, the new fun sound.

I love to play and twist and shout

For that's what life is all about.

Join with me you happy crowd

And play the music fast and loud.

Name

A STORY OR POEM
I HAVE ENJOYED READING

Use these headings to write about a story or poem you have enjoyed reading. Say why you like it.

Title
By

Kind of story or poem

What it is about?

Characters

Where and when it is set

Mood of the story or poem

Style or way in which it is written

Why I like it

English KS2 Master File © E J P & D C P

Name

TRAVELLING BY TRAIN

1. Look at the illustration below of a train at a station.
2. Read the poem. Say why you like or dislike it.
3. What part of the poem is illustrated by the picture?
4. Find two things in the picture which show that this is a recent drawing.
5. Write a poem about a journey you have made.
6. Tell a story beginning
'We arrived at our station at 12.15pm. Aunt Miriam had been waiting for us and shepherded us into the waiting taxi. Our luggage was put in the front and we were off...

> Fast as lightning, smooth as silk,
> Trains, passengers, post and milk,
> Up the mountains, down the dales
> Into Scotland, England and Wales.
> Station's near, brakes shriek, stopping times,
> Arrivals, departures, cases and signs.
> (Deborah, aged 11)

Name _____

WHAT HAPPENS NEXT?

Read the passages below and then write what you think happens next. Draw a picture/s to illustrate the story.

> Jane and Robert were walking in the Scottish Highlands. When they set out, the morning had been bright and sunny and they had made good progress. In the middle of the morning, they stopped near a hill fort and ate the sandwiches they had brought with them for lunch. They were sure they would find an inn or farmhouse where they could have a midday meal. Jane drew some of the wildflowers in her sketch book and Robert, a history student, wandered off to explore the site.

OR

> Time passed quickly as Robert took photographs and made notes. Occasionally, he looked back at Jane who had fallen asleep. He began to feel hungry. The sun was hidden by clouds and a cool breeze made him remember the warm pullover he had decided not to bring. It was time to have lunch and then make their way home. In minutes, the breeze stiffened and the first specks of rain fell. Head bent he walked back to where he had left Jane. There was only her sketch book which Robert picked up calling her name. There was no answer.

> Time passed quickly as Jane sketched and photographed the flowers. The sun was warm on her face and she lay back feeling sleepy.
> Heavy rain woke her. Distant lightning streaked the dark sky and thunder rumbled over the hills. Within minutes she was soaked to the skin. Quickly, she scrambled towards the ruins of the fort, calling for Robert. There was no answer.

Robert . . .

Jane . . .

Name _____

WHAT HAPPENED BEFORE?

Read the passage at the bottom of the page. Suggest what happened before.
Draw a picture/s to illustrate the story.

'We should have hidden in the lifeboats instead,' said William. 'Now that we have been found out, we'll probably be clapped in irons or flogged or something even worse.'

He remembered a story in which pirates had tied a castaway to the mast of the ship and left him there while the ship sailed through a storm.

His older brother Malcolm did not agree, but he too, was very frightened at the consequences of their actions. It had seemed exciting last night, a real adventure.

The sun was high in the sky and the boys could not see properly, but the man coming towards them was a giant and curiously familiar.

'What are you doing here? Everyone's been looking for you all night and your mother and father are frantic with worry.'

To his dismay, William began to cry, the tears making channels in the dirt on his face.

'There's no need for that,' said Uncle Bill gruffly. 'Your parents are so worried you'll probably get off lightly.'

Bending down, he picked up William then took Malcolm's hand.

'It's time to go home.'

English KS2 Master File © E J P & D C P   Reading/What Happened Before? 42

Name _____

MISSING WORDS

Find the missing words.

PACKING A PRESENT

Wrap the present in tissue _____. Place in a strong cardboard _____. Wrap the box in _____ paper. Cut a length of _____ using a _____. Tie the _____ around the _____. Write the _____ and _____ on a label and _____ it on the parcel. Take it to the _____ _____.

TO MAKE GARLIC MUSHROOMS

Martha liked to cook. She lived in a cottage near the sea and this is one of her favourite recipes.

Melt 50 g butter in a frying _____. Finely chop 4 spring onions. Crush 2 cloves of garlic. Fry the o _____ and g _____ in the b _____ until soft. Remove from the heat and stir in 100 g breadc _____. Chop 2 tablespoons of f _____ parsley and s _____ into the mixture. Season with _____ and _____. Brush a shallow tin with 1 tablespoon of olive _____ Remove the stalks from 24 cup mushrooms and fill with the g _____ mixture. Stand the mushrooms in the t _____. Sprinkle over the rest of the olive _____ and cover with foil. Bake for 25 - 30 m _____ in a moderately hot oven (190°C, 375°F, gas mark 5). Remove the f _____ for the last 5 m _____. Serve h _____.

Draw a picture of Martha cooking in the kitchen in her cottage.

Name _____

THE DEWEY SYSTEM

This is a summary of the Dewey book classification system used in most public libraries. In this system, different kinds of books are given different numbers.

Numbers between

- 000 - 099 General books including encyclopaedias.
- 100 - 199 Philosophical books (books containing serious discussions about the meaning of life, religion and the world.)
- 200 - 299 Religious books.
- 300 - 399 Social sciences (the study of society and people), law, education and money matters.
- 400 - 499 Language, grammar, dictionaries, word collections.
- 500 - 599 The sciences - chemistry, physics, biology, mathematics.
- 600 - 699 Technology - engineering, medicine, agriculture, computing.
- 700 - 799 The arts - painting, music, sculpture, recreation.
- 800 - 899 Literature - great literary works, plays.
- 900 - 999 History, geography.

In which of the Dewey classifications would you find books with the following titles? The first one has been done for you.

Title	Classification
1. 'The Vikings'	900 - 999
2. 'Parliament and People'	
3. 'Elementary Mathematics'	
4. 'Teaching Reading'	
5. 'Famous Paintings'	
6. 'Music for the Masses'	
7. 'A Christmas Carol' by Charles Dickens	
8. 'Macbeth' by William Shakespeare	
9. 'The Structure of Plants'	
10. 'The Use of Drugs in Hospitals'	
11. 'Great Musicians'	
12. 'How a Computer Works'	
13. 'Looking at the Stars in the Sky'	
14 'Strange Customs'	
15 'Castles in England and Wales'	

WHERE CAN I FIND IT?

Where would you find the information or places in the column on the left? Possible answers are given at the bottom of the page but not in the correct order. The first one has been done for you

A person's account of his or her own life	Autobiography
A telephone number	
A fax number	
The routes and times of trains	
The meanings of words	
The location of a town	
The list of members of a class	
The days and months of a year	
The time of day	
Lists of words similar to others in meaning	
A place where you can borrow books	
A place where you can borrow records	
A place where you can rent videos	
A machine which records data	
Records of recent events	
General knowledge	
A place where paintings are exhibited	
A record of a person's everyday life	
An account of a person's life	
A collection of poems	
A list of voters	
Details of what a book contains	
An alphabetical list of the subjects in a book	
A list of books used in research	
Annual calendar of natural events	

Choose your answers from this list.

Almanac	class register	fax directory	record library
anthology	clock	glossary	telephone directory
art gallery	computer	index	television
atlas	contents	library	thesaurus
autobiography	diary	museum	train time-table
bibliography	dictionary	newspaper	video library
biography	electoral register	radio	video shop
calendar	encyclopaedia		

IN THE KITCHEN

Look quickly at the picture then answer these questions.

1. Where is the picture set?
2. How many people are there in the picture?
3. How many animals are there in the picture?
4. What is the woman doing?
5. What is the boy doing?
6. What is the man doing?
7. What is the dog doing?
8. What is the dog's name?
9. What is the cat doing?
10. What animal is in the basket?
11. What time of day do you think it is?

Name

ON THE FARM

Look quickly at the picture then answer these questions.

1. How many people are in the picture?
2. What is the boy at the bottom of the picture doing?
3. What is the farmer going to do?
4. What is the girl doing?
5. How many pigs are there?
6. What are the pigs doing?
7. Are the wheels of the tractor all the same size?
8. How many sheep are there in the picture?
9. What is the cockerel in the picture doing?
10. How many cows can you see?
11. What time of year do you think it is?

English KS2 Master File © E J P & D C P   Reading/The Farmyard 47

Name _____

FINDING OUT

This is a short extract from a local telephone directory.

Hopkins Arthur, 25 Brynteg Lane 017 334
Hopkins Brinley, Estate Agents, 84 Hazel Road 017 459
Hopkins Charles, Hair by Charles, 63 Heather Crescent 017 831
Hopkins Mrs Dilys, 10 Jones Terrace 017 452
Hopkins Edward, Dental Surgeon, 30 Gurnos Place 017 353
Hopkins Fred, Furniture Removals, 36 Ruskin Street 017 632
Hopkins Harry, 62 Orchard Lane 017 223
Hopkins Isaac, The Happy Restaurant, 4 Villiers Mews 017 555
Hopkins James, 30 The Kingsway 017 106
Hopkins Joseph, The George Leisure Centre, The Promenade 017 705
Hopkins Dr Len,
   Surgery, 10 Phoenix Way 017 604
   Residence, 4 Cameron Boulevard 017 721

Answer the following questions using the information above. The first one has been done for you.

1. What is Arthur Hopkins' telephone number?   017 334
2. In what order are the names listed?
3. Where does Edward Hopkins live? What is his telephone number?
4. You are looking for a new flat. Where would you go for information about one?
5. You want to move your belongings into a new flat. What number would you ring to arrange help with this?
6. Mrs Hopkins lives at 10 Jones Terrace. What is her Christian name?
7. You have broken a tooth? What number would you ring for help?
8. You want to play badminton with your friends. What is the name of the Leisure Centre? What number would you ring to book a court?
9. Your mother is organising a birthday treat for you and your friends at the Happy Restaurant. What number will she ring? What is the address of the restaurant?
10. What is the profession of Len Hopkins? Where does he live and what is his telephone number? Where is his surgery and what is its telephone number?

English KS2 Master File © E J P & D C P   Reading/Finding Out 48

Name _____

IN HOSPITAL

Operations are performed in an operating theatre.

This man is having an operation.

There is a very bright light above the operating table so that the surgeon can see clearly.

The patient is given a gas to make him sleep (an anaesthetic) and oxygen for him to breathe.

The patient may also be given drugs intravenously (on a 'drip').

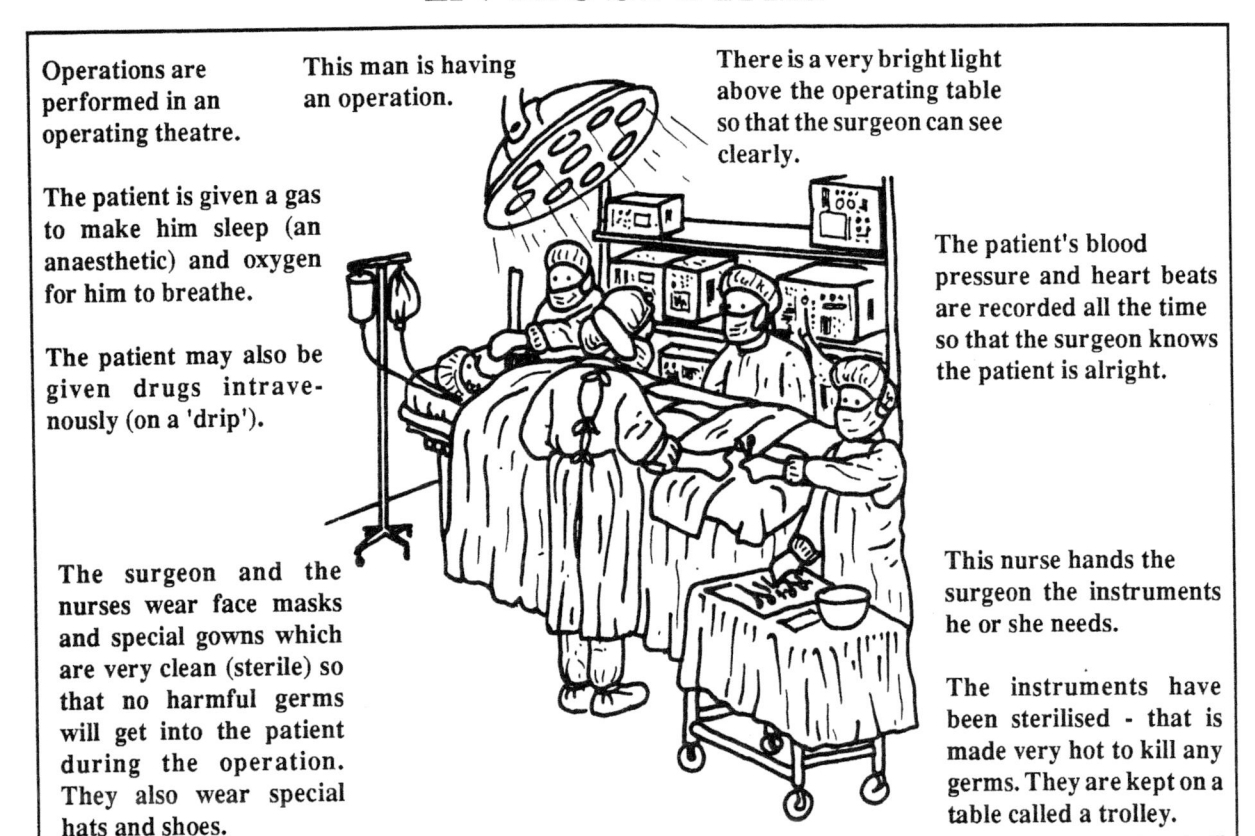

The patient's blood pressure and heart beats are recorded all the time so that the surgeon knows the patient is alright.

The surgeon and the nurses wear face masks and special gowns which are very clean (sterile) so that no harmful germs will get into the patient during the operation. They also wear special hats and shoes.

This nurse hands the surgeon the instruments he or she needs.

The instruments have been sterilised - that is made very hot to kill any germs. They are kept on a table called a trolley.

1. What is the name of a doctor who performs operations?
2. Doctors and nurses wear special clothes in an operating theatre. What are they?
3. Why do doctors and nurses wear special clothes in an operating theatre?
4. What is meant by 'sterilised'?
5. What makes a patient sleep throughout an operation?
6. Why is oxygen given to the patient?
7. Why does the nurse hand the instruments to the surgeon?
8. Why is there a very bright light in the operating theatre?
9. What are the containers on the stand to the left of the picture used for?
10. The patient's _____ and _____ are measured all the time. Why is this necessary?

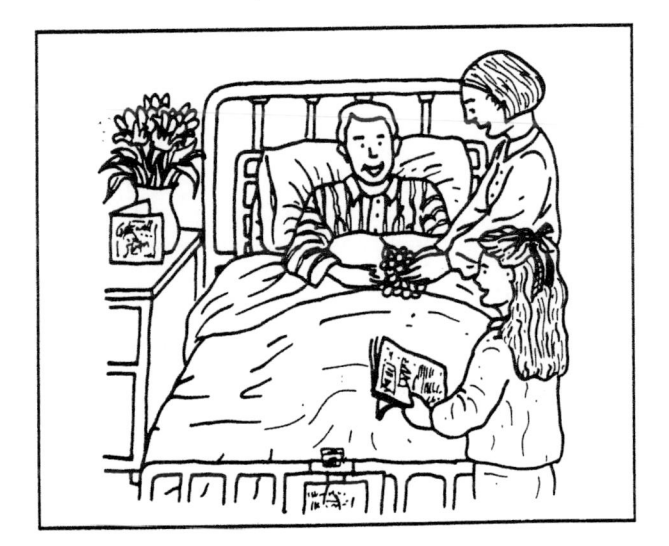

In this picture, the man is much better after his operation and is sitting up in bed. His wife and daughter have come to visit him. What have they brought him? Why do you think they chose these gifts?

What do you think they are talking about?

Name

BOOKSHELF

Write about a favourite book on your bookshelf or one that you have read recently.

1. Title and Author.

2. Kind of book.

3. Outline of the plot. How it begins and how it ends.

4. The main characters.

5. Ways in which the author describes the characters.

6. Ways in which the author develops the story.

7. Ways in which the author creates the atmosphere of the story.

8. How it compares with other stories by the same author.

9. What I think of the book.

10. Draw a picture about the story or one of the characters in the book.

English KS2 Master File © E J P & D C P

Reading/Bookshelf 50

Name _____

FACTS OR OPINIONS?

Decide if the following sentences are facts or opinions. In each case, draw a circle around the word or words which show the sentence is a fact and a square around the word or words which show the sentence is an opinion.

1. My dad's car is red.

2. Jones the Baker is the best baker in town.

3. Rachel has long hair.

4. Jane has two brothers.

5. Our house is the finest in the street.

6. The rose is the most beautiful flower.

7. Paul is the happiest boy in the class.

8. It's John's birthday today.

9. Aunt Sarah is the kindest lady in the world.

10. Harry is a computer operator.

Sarah and Robert are talking about a mutual friend, Timothy.

Sarah: I'm going to ask Tim to my birthday party.

Robert: Fine. I hope he's better behaved than he was the last time.

Sarah: What do you mean? That was just an accident.

Robert: Accident or not, he caused a lot of fuss and we were ages cleaning up. Dad was furious and said I wasn't to have anything more to do with him.

Sarah: But you're often with Tim. I've seen you.

Robert: I know. It's difficult to avoid someone who lives next door and does the same subjects in school.

Sarah: Does that mean that if I ask Tim you won't come to my party?

How do you think Robert will answer Sarah's question?
Do Sarah and Robert both like or dislike Timothy?
What do you think the 'accident' was?
Give reasons for your opinions.

Name _____

ADVERTISEMENTS

Advertisers try to persuade us to buy things. Sometimes they give information about the products or services they are trying to sell. Is this information always accurate?

What do you think is being advertised in these pictures? How do you know what the advertisers are saying?

Make up your own advertisement. Remember some have sequels or a story line or characters that link a series of advertisements. Some involve famous people.

English KS2 Master File © E J P & D C P   Reading/Advertisements 52

Name _____

RESEARCH PROJECT 1

Fnding out all you can about a topic can be interesting and exciting especially if you can choose the subject yourself. Use all the information available in the school library, the general library and write for leaflets. It is important to know how many words are needed. Suppose you had to write about

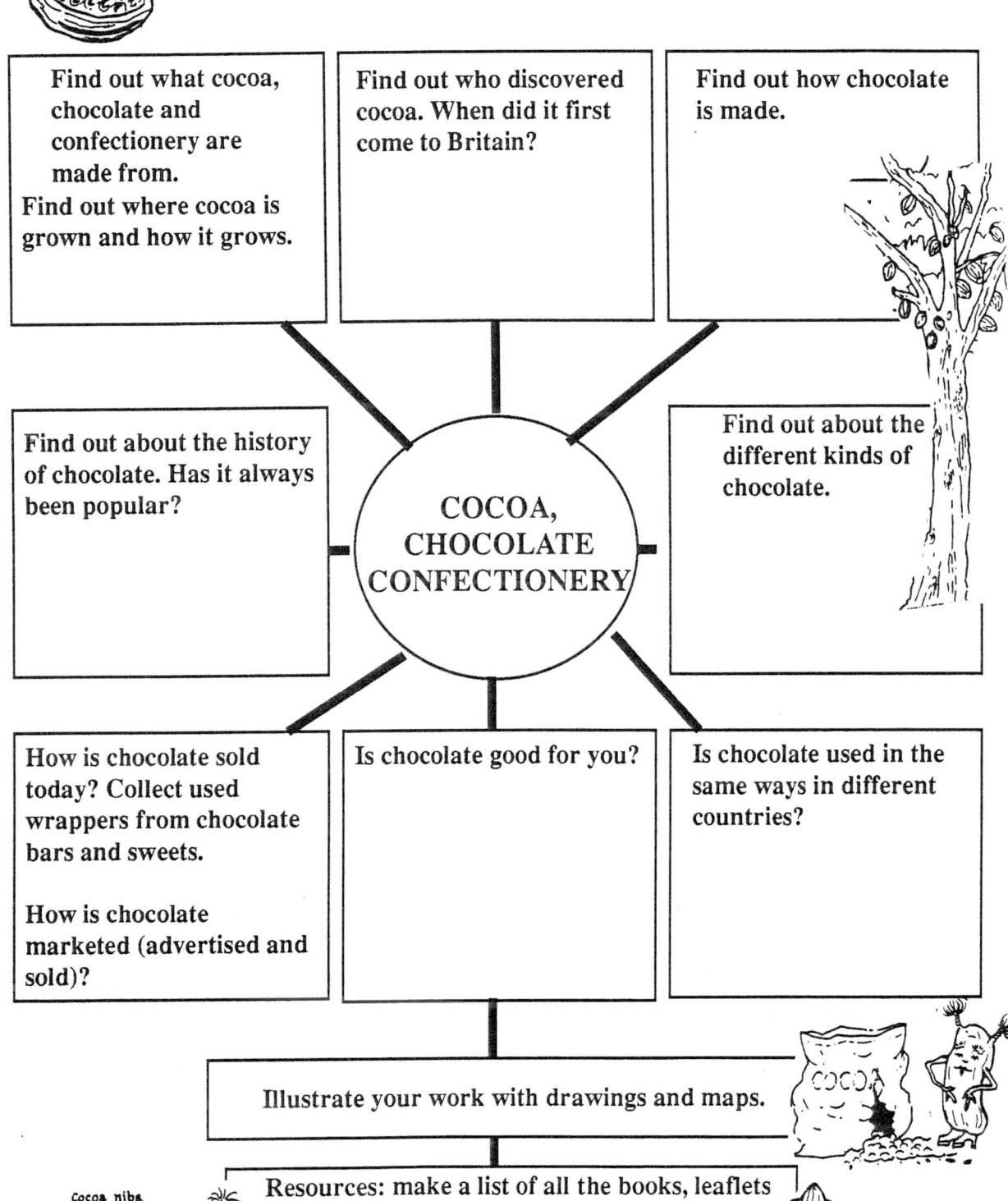

COCOA, CHOCOLATE AND CONFECTIONERY.

- Find out what cocoa, chocolate and confectionery are made from.
  Find out where cocoa is grown and how it grows.

- Find out who discovered cocoa. When did it first come to Britain?

- Find out how chocolate is made.

- Find out about the history of chocolate. Has it always been popular?

COCOA, CHOCOLATE CONFECTIONERY

- Find out about the different kinds of chocolate.

- How is chocolate sold today? Collect used wrappers from chocolate bars and sweets.

  How is chocolate marketed (advertised and sold)?

- Is chocolate good for you?

- Is chocolate used in the same ways in different countries?

Illustrate your work with drawings and maps.

Resources: make a list of all the books, leaflets and other sources/contacts you have used.

Do not eat all the samples collected for your research!

English KS2 Master File © E J P & D C P   Reading/Research Project 1 53

Name _____

RESEARCH PROJECT 2

THE LIFE OF A FAMOUS PERSON

Use an encyclopaedia, books, local libraries and museums. Sometimes there are societies organised in the name of a famous person. Other books/articles may have been written about him or her before.

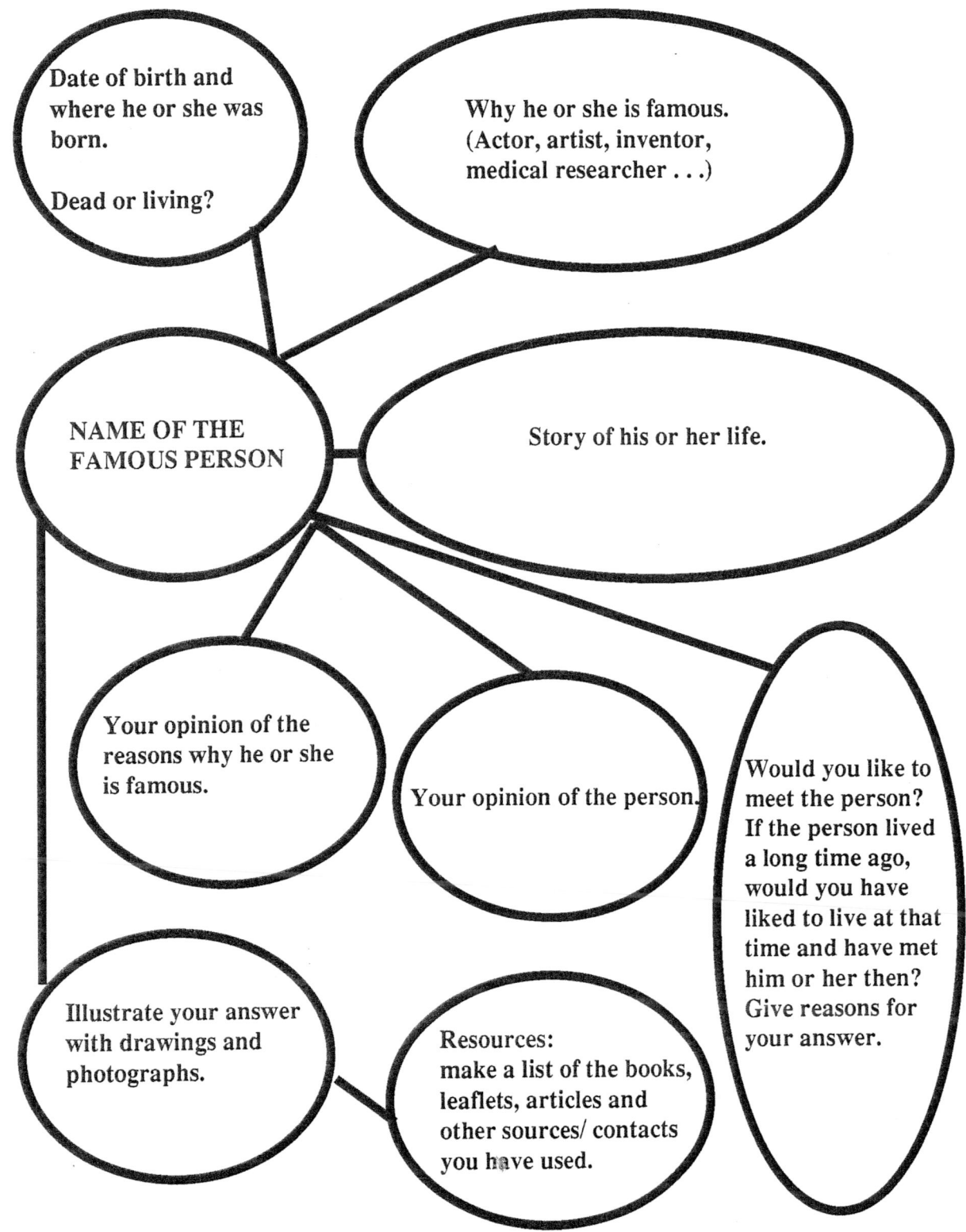

- Date of birth and where he or she was born. Dead or living?

- Why he or she is famous. (Actor, artist, inventor, medical researcher . . .)

- NAME OF THE FAMOUS PERSON

- Story of his or her life.

- Your opinion of the reasons why he or she is famous.

- Your opinion of the person.

- Would you like to meet the person? If the person lived a long time ago, would you have liked to live at that time and have met him or her then? Give reasons for your answer.

- Illustrate your answer with drawings and photographs.

- Resources: make a list of the books, leaflets, articles and other sources/ contacts you have used.

Name _____

THE RIGHT WORD

Choose the best word from each of the pairs given in the following passages. Give each passage a title.

One of the big problems/difficulties facing the universe/world today is the many/number of species/kinds of animals in danger/harm of becoming dead/extinct. One of the most usual/obvious causes of extinction is chasing/hunting. Once man killed wild animals for food now it is for their skins and horns. Today, animals are helped/threatened by the changing/destruction of their habitats, for example the trimming/felling of tropical rainforests/farms.

Today, when people fly everywhere/elsewhere, it is easy/hard to realise that until recently/soonest it was needless/necessary to travel by ship for any journey overseas. It is still always/often easier to send freight/equipment by water except for perished/perishable goods which must travel more slowly/quickly.

History is the tale/story of people and what they did in the present/past. Important events/happenings extinguish/distinguish one period of history from another. Peasants/rulers exerted enormous influence/pressure on their peoples/races. People grew/developed at different times. They were incapable/unable to record what was happening until the invention/discovery of writing about 5,500 years ago.

This is a list of different kinds of housing.
Match each word with its correct description.

1. Cottage
2. Bungalow
3. Terraced house
4. Semi-detached house
5. Mansion
6. Hovel

A. A house joined to others in a row.
B. A house with all the rooms on the ground floor.
C. A large house usually owned by rich people.
D. A small house usually in the country.
E. A very poor, ramshackled dwelling.
F. A house joined to one other house only.

THE CROCODILE

Draw a picture to illustrate this poem.
Where do you think the writer was when he fell?
Give one word to describe the crocodile.

While up aloft the wind was high, it blew a gale from the south,
I lost my hold and away did fly right into the crocodile's mouth,
He quickly closed his jaws on me and thought he'd got a victim,
But I ran down his throat, d'ye see, and that's the way I tricked him.

The crocodile being very old, one day, alas, he died;
He was ten long years a-getting cold, he was so long and wide.
His skin was eight miles thick, I'm sure, or very near about,
For I was full ten years or more a-cutting my way out.

                                                            Anonymous

Name _____

THE BIG ROCK CANDY MOUNTAINS

Draw a picture to illustrate this poem.
What sort of land is described in the poem?
Would you like to go there? Give reasons for your answer.

> In the Big Rock Candy Mountains,
> All the cops have wooden legs,
> The bulldogs all have rubber teeth,
> And the hens lay soft-boiled eggs,
> The farmers' trees are full of fruit,
> And the barns are full of hay.
> Oh, I'm bound to go where there ain't no snow,
> Where the rain don't pour, the wind don't blow,
> In the Big Rock Candy Mountains.
>   Anonymous

Write a poem or a short story about this visitor.

Name _____

SENTENCES 1

Here are the endings of ten sentences.

A. ... piano.

B. ... the dripping tap.

C. ... the picture.

D. ... 100 pages.

E. ... wagged its tail.

F. ... flew high above the trees.

G. ... the tractor across the field.

H. ... the bird.

I. ... back on the shelf.

J. ... noisily out of the station.

Here are ten beginnings of sentences. Complete them using the endings above.
The first one has been done for you.

1. The cat chased the bird.

2. The music teacher played the _____

3. The engine steamed _____

4. The plumber mended _____

5. The artist painted _____

6. The librarian put the books _____

7. The book has _____

8. The dog _____

9. The bird _____

10. The farmer drove _____

Name _____

SENTENCES 2

A capital letter is used at the beginning of a sentence and a full stop at the end.

1. Put the capital letters and full stops in these sentences.
   the horse jumped the fence
   the hen laid an egg
   we had cakes for tea
   the sea was cold
   the sun shone brightly

2. The words in these sentences are in the wrong order. Write them out in the correct order with a capital at the beginning of each sentence and a full stop at the end.

   keep farmers cows for their milk
   by barking was the gate the dog
   to milk drink a cat loves a saucer of
   noisily the house zoomed over the aeroplane
   my favourite chicken is meal and chips
   sums marked the teacher all my right
   the bandaged nurse grazed my elbow
   the swam bowl goldfish round and round its

3. Put full stops and capital letters in this passage.

all the animals on the farm were asleep except the owl suddenly it saw the fox creeping towards the hen house looking for his dinner the owl hooted loudly all the animals woke up the farm dog chased the fox away soon all the animals were asleep again

3. Give this picture a title then write five sentences about it.

English KS2 Master File © E J P & D C P   Writing/Sentences 2 59

Name _____

NOUNS

Common nouns are the names of things or animals.

Draw a circle around the common nouns in this passage.

The engine huffed and puffed as it pulled the carriages up the hill. The engine driver shovelled more coal into the boiler and pulled the whistle. Some sheep sleeping in the field ran away frightened by the noise. The little engine took no notice. The sun was shining. It was a lovely day.

Proper nouns are the names of people or places. They have capital letters.

Some proper and common nouns have been mixed up. Can you separate them into two lists? One in each group has been done for you.

COMMON NOUNS	Jill boy London girl Christmas rabbit February car Denmark Wednesday train butterfly Pembroke Castle steam money Mr Morgan day Orchard Lane Edward baker Mrs Lewis water	PROPER NOUNS
boy		Jill

THE GUNPOWDER PLOT

Draw circles around the proper nouns in these sentences.

1. On November 5th. 1605, Guy Fawkes tried to blow up Parliament.

2. He was angry about the harsh laws passed by King James 1st.

3. He hid explosives under the House of Lords.

4. He waited for all the Members of the House of Commons to meet.

5. Fortunately, he was discovered by soldiers of the King and arrested.

6. Guy Fawkes was tried for treason then hanged, drawn and quartered.

7. Today, we remember Guy Fawkes with fireworks and bonfires on November 5th.

English KS2 Master File © E J P & D C P

DOING WORDS 1

Verbs are doing words or action words.
Draw a circle around the doing words in the following sentences.

1. The boys race down the road.
2. The hen lays an egg.
3. The cat sleeps in the sun.
4. John threw the ball.
5. Louise read the book.
6. The goldfish swims in the tank.
7. The school choir sang in the concert.
8. My mother made a new dress for me.
9. The tiny bird flies from the nest.
10. The boys played football in the field.

Match these noises and the things that make them.

sizzle	clock
rumbles	steam engine
howls	stairs
creak	mud
rings	thunder
ticks	wind
whirrs	bell
splatters	hands
clap	spinning top
puffs	sausages

COCK A DOODLE MOO
What sounds do these animals make?

Name _____

DOING WORDS 2

1. Use these doing words in these sentences.

   polish
   take
   writing
   sing
   baked

   1. I like to _____ with the choir.
   2. Clean your shoes and then _____ them.
   3. _____ the dog for a walk.
   4. Mum _____ a cake for tea.
   5. I am _____ a letter to my friend.

2. Which of the following are sentences and which are phrases? Underline the sentences and write them out with capitals and full stops.

   1. comb your hair
   2. it comes naturally to him
   3. at the bus stop
   4. meet me at the station
   5. one morning in June
   6. i like kippers for tea
   7. he slithered to a stop
   8. good gracious me
   9. after the match
   10. lay the table for breakfast
   11. my friend Susan
   12. the long and short of it
   13. he was quietly confident
   14. the final score at the end
   15. there are field mice in the garden
   16. snow is white and very cold
   17. the ugly bear in the zoo
   18. use the scissors to cut paper
   19. at the jeweller's in the main street
   20. bring your work with you

3. Write five sentences about this picture.

Name

INFORMATION SENTENCES

1. Read the following passage and then answer the questions below.

   There is nothing at all wrong with wearing T-shirts. They are inexpensive, comfortable and if kept clean they are attractive. They can be easily washed and take a long time to wear out. Some have strange drawings, pictures, logos or slogans on them. These are a matter of personal taste. Some of these embellishments are merely decorative, others express an opinon, while others advertise a variety of things such as 'pop' groups, soft drinks or places. I am in favour of T-shirts, especially on holiday.

   1. How many words are there in the first sentence?
   2. What is the passage about?
   3. Give five reasons why T-shirts are good to wear.
   4. When does the writer thing it is most appropriate to wear a T-shirt?
   5. What is meant by 'a long time to wear out'?
   6. What is usually found on T-shirts?
   7. What is meaning of 'embellishments', 'merely decorative', 'express an opinion', 'advertise a variety of things'?
   8. Does the writer think T-shirts are 'good value for money'? Give reasons for your answer.
   9. Why are T-shirts so called?
   10. Describe your favourite T-shirt.

2. Design a T-shirt and give reasons for your choice of design.

3. Put these sentences in the correct order.
   Begin with
   One day I baked a cake.

   I poured the mixture into a cake tin.
   When the cake was cooked, I cut it it into slices for tea.
   I mixed all the ingredients together in a bowl.
   I baked the cake in the oven.
   I weighed all the ingredients.
   The cake was delicious.
   I went to the shop and bought the things I needed.

4. Join these sentences together. You may need to change some of the words.
   Do not use the same joining word more than once.
   1. Martin drew a picture.   Martin painted it.
   2. John could not go to the cinema.   John was too young.
   3. Mary broke the toy.   Mary must mend it.
   4. Eric's room was untidy.   Eric's mother told him to tidy it.
   5. The boy looked both ways.   He crossed the road.
   6. James won the tennis match.   James was injured.
   7. Colin is the brave boy.   Colin rescued the dog.
   8. Jennifer bought a coat.   Jennifer bought a pair of shoes.
   9. It was snowing.   We went skiing.
   10. Timothy's mother gave him an ice cream. Timothy ate the ice cream.

Joining words to use: so, and, because, then, which, although, who, before, when, next.

Name

DESCRIBING WORDS 1

1. Write captions under these drawings using the lists of nouns and describing words.

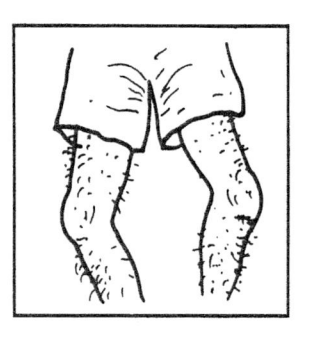

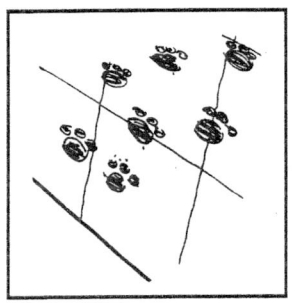

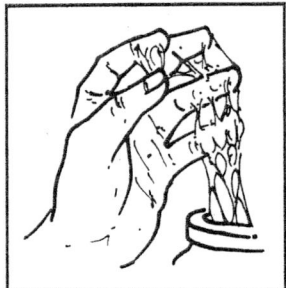

red			paws
muddy			wind
slimy			knife
sticky			legs
white			fire engine
whistling			bear
sharp			top
buzzing			fingers
cuddly			saucer
bandy			snail
spinning			bee
flying			snow

2. Adjectives are describing words. Choose three describing words to go with each of the nouns.

an egg	glamorous, blonde, talented
an orange	sweet, thick-skinned, juicy
a 'pop' star	crowded, red, late
a bus	short, funny, exciting
a puppy	brown, hardboiled, fresh
a story	wet-nosed, brown eyed, long-tailed

English KS2 Master File © E J P & D C P   Writing/Describing Words 1   64

Name _____

DESCRIBING WORDS 2

1. Describe yourself or your friend.

Name
Face, hair, eyes, smile
Tall, short, fat, thin . . .
Character, jolly, shy, timid, clever, dull, kind, thoughtful . . .
Special characteristics
Things I (or my friend) like to do most
What I like/dislike most about myself (or my friend)

2. Write 5 sentences to describe each of the following.
   A walk along the beach early in the morning.
   Christmas shopping.   A puppy.
   A bike you want to sell.   Your favourite piece of music.

3. Write 5 sentences to describe this picture.

English KS2 Master File © E J P & D C P   Writing/Describing Words 2

Name

ADVERBS

1. An adverb tells you more about the meaning of a verb. Draw a circle around the adverbs in these sentences.

1. The baby cried loudly.
2. The giant stamped heavily.
3. The gymnast jumped high over the rope.
4. I'm running quickly.
5. The light shone brightly.
6. The Princess laughed happily.
7. The goat trembled fearfully.
8. The limpet was stuck hard and fast.
9. Go away.
10. The baby slept peacefully.

2. Match these verbs and adverbs.

clap	fretfully
run	bravely
gaze	heavily
hug	longingly
whisper	rudely
fight	quietly
worry	helplessly
ignore	fast
trip	loudly
giggle	warmly

3. Suggest 3 adverbs to use with each of these verbs.

Tremble, whimper, scream, touch, slither, climb, hurry, crawl, scrape, whisper.

4. Fill the spaces with suitable adverbs.

The moon shone _____ between the _____ moving clouds. The leaves rustled _____ in the evening breeze. Jane shivered and pulled her shawl _____ around her. Shadows of the trees danced _____ and _____ she felt _____ frightened. If she was found _____ she would be beaten _____ . At last she found the heavy gate. It opened _____ and she stumbled _____ into the arms of her friend.

5. You are a sports reporter for the local paper. Write an account of a local derby football or rugby match.

QUESTIONS 1

1. Today, you interviewed a beautiful young girl. These are the answers she gave to your questions. Write the questions you asked. Remember to add question marks.

1.	1. My name is Cinderella.
2.	2. I live with my stepmother and two ugly sisters.
3.	3. I have to do all the cleaning.
4.	4. Yes, it is very hard work.
5.	5. Last night I went to a ball at the palace.
6.	6. I danced with the Prince.
7.	7. I left at midnight.
8.	8. Because after that my coach would have changed into a pumpkin.
9.	9. Yes. I lost my glass slipper.
10.	10. No. I didn't know the Prince had found it.
11.	11. No. The Prince has not come here yet.

2. Suggest five reasons why the story of Cinderella remains a favourite with young children. Is it at all like 'real life'? Give reasons for your answer.

Name _____

QUESTIONS 2

1. Change these indirect questions into direct ones.

1. She asked if he had read 'A Christmas Carol' by Charles Dickens.
2. He wondered if she had seen the film.
3. Jane asked her friend if she would like to go to the beach.
4. He wanted to know the age of the tree.
5. He enquired about the time of the next train.
6. The porter asked if he could help with the luggage.
7. He needed to know how much paint he should buy.
8. He wondered who would win.
9. He wished to know if his friend was better.
10. The waiter asked if they were enjoying their meal.

2. There is a new girl or boy in your class. What questions will you ask the newcomer?

3. You are booking a holiday through a travel agent. You have never been to the place before. What questions would you ask the travel agent?

4. You have been asked to attend an interview for a job that you would really like.

   Write 5 questions you would expect to be asked at the interview.
   How would you answer?

   Write 3 questions you would ask at the interview.

> Useful question words and phrases.
>
> How? When? Why? How much? Can we? What? What if? What next?
> May we? What happens if? Is there another? How far? Where? Who?

Name _____

PUNCTUATION

1. Write out the book covers for the following stories. Put in the capitals and full stops.

    invaders from outer space by a m strange

    party cakes by john lewis

    life in a submarine by d b bell

    my favourite sport by archibald bones

    ghost stories by w h ghoul

2. Put capitals, full stops and commas in this passage.

many different plants live on the rocky shores where the hard rocks of the land meet the sea seaweeds limpets barnacles and snails live there in the crevices pools and among the boulders formed by the rocks when you lift up a rock always put it back gently in case you injure any defenceless creatures.

3. Put capitals in this passage.

    mum said, 'you must tidy your room before you go out.'

    'i shall be late,' i pointed out.

    dad said, 'you should have thought of that before. i haven't got time to do it for you.'

    'could i do it tomorrow, please? i promise to do it,' i begged.

    mum said, 'very well. but don't let me down.'

4. Write abbreviations for the following. Remember to put in the full stops.

    | doctor | street | metre | mistress |
    | saint | south west | year | plural |
    | road | kilogram | mister | singular |

5. Fnd the missing letters and write the words in full.

    | can't | I'll | she's | he's |
    | won't | what's | it's | I've |
    | haven't | I'm | let's | they'd |

English KS2 Master File © E J P & D C P   Writing/Punctuation 69

Name _____

SENTENCES 3

1. Draw circles around the subjects and squares around the predicates in these sentences.

    1. Jane washed her T-shirt in hot soapy water.

    2. The carpenter made new bookshelves.

    3. The girl caught the ball.

    4. The teacher marked all the papers.

    5. Louise sewed a patch on her jeans.

2. Add subjects to these predicates.

    1. _____ played rugby.

    2. _____ jumped the fence.

    3. _____ took my temperature.

    4. _____ mended the dripping tap.

3. Add predicates to these subjects.

    1. The two friends _____

    2. The sports teacher _____

    3. The bird _____

    4. The artist _____

4. Write each of these sentences in a different way. You may have to change the words slightly but the meaning should remain the same.

    1. Jamie missed the bus because he was late.

    2. It had started to rain when Margaret left the shop.

    3. Bill walked quickly to school.

    4. Rosemary played her best and so won the match.

    5. Tim was tired and cross and shouted at his little brother.

Name _____

LAYOUT

1. Match these beginnings and endings of letters.

   Dear Aunt Agatha,

   Dear Sir,

   Dear Mr Williams,

   My dearest Tom,

   Dear Old Thing,

   Yours faithfully,
   Jennifer Jones.

   Love,
   Jane.

   Your affectionate nephew,
   George.

   Bye for now,
   Bill.

   Yours sincerely,
   Elizabeth Ellis.

2. Read this invitation to a party and then answer the questions.

   > 4, Laburnum Rd.,
   > Apple Centre,
   > Littlehampton LT1.
   > 5. 8. 19 . . .
   >
   > Dear Colin,
   >   Just a note to ask you to my birthday party on Thursday, the 24th. of August at 2.30 - 5.00 pm. Mum has hired the church hall at the end of our road and we should have a great time.
   >
   >   John.
   >
   > RSVP

   1. Where does the writer live?
   2. When is the party?
   3. Where is the party?
   4. How long is the party expected to last?
   5. What does RSVP mean?
   6. Address the envelope containing your reply to Colin Morgan.

3. Write a letter to your Aunt Agatha, thanking her for the Christmas present she sent to you.

Name _____

LIFE IN A CASTLE

1. Suggest another title for this piece.

2. Put in sub-headings and punctuation marks.

Girls and boys born to noble families had special rights and responsibilities in castle life Girls had two choices they could either marry or become nuns Most were married by the time they were fourteen Girls were taught by nuns how to be a lady-in-waiting or how to be a good wife for a baron If a young girl did not want to marry or no one wanted to marry her then she could choose between a number of nunneries throughout the country Women were not allowed to go to university and could not become doctors Most of them could not read or write A noblewoman had to look after a large household She had to instruct staff organise meals and manage the budget A craftsman's wife was expected to help him at his work although she was paid about half as much as he for the same work Boys were often placed in a neighbouring baron's household These youngsters might train as pages who served one or perhaps two knights They began their day by helping their masters to dress After breakfast they would be taught reading writing and Latin by one of the chaplain's priests These classes might be followed by singing and dancing classes They practised fighting wih light wooden swords and might also help with hunting and hawking When he became older a boy usually became a knight's squire Eventually he would become a knight Boys who did not train for a military life might be sent to an abbey or cathedral school to be trained to become priests or for administrative and clerical work They could become officials at the king's court or lawyers or officials in the law courts

3. Answer these questions on the above passage.

1. Girls had two choices, what were they?
2. What skills would be learnt by the daughter of a nobleman?
3. According to the passage, what were women not allowed to do?
4. Why do you think most women could not read or write?
5. If a woman did not marry, what did she do?
6. What were the duties of a noblewoman?
7. How and where were young boys trained for military life?
8. What were the duties of a young boy?
9. What were the duties of a squire?
10. If a young boy did not want to become a knight, what did he do?

Name _____

THE 'ROYAL GEORGE'
FOUR THINGS

1. These are three verses from 'The Loss of the Royal George' by William Cowper. There are four lines to each verse. Write out the verses and put in the necessary punctuation.

   toll for the brave the brave that are no more all sunk beneath the wave fast by their native shore eight hundred of the brave whose courage well was tried had made the vessel heel and laid her on her side a land-breeze shook the shrouds and she was overset down went the royal george with all her crew complete

   What was the 'Royal George'?

   What happened to the 'Royal George'?

   How many men were lost?

   What is a shroud?

   What does 'a land-breeze shook the shrouds' mean in the poem?

   [This is based on a true disaster in Portsmouth harbour. In fact the bottom of the 'Royal George' was rotten and fell out. Cowper did not know this when he wrote the poem.]

2. This extract from 'The Book of Proverbs' has five lines. Write it out correctly and put in the necessary punctuation.

   there be four things which are little upon the earth but they are exceeding wise the ants are a people not strong yet they prepare their meat in the summer the conies are but a feeble folk yet make their houses in the rocks the locusts have no king yet they go forth all of them by bands the spider taketh hold with her hands and is in king's palaces

   Conies are rabbits, what are the other three creatures mentioned in the passage?

   In what way is each of the four creatures in the passage wise?

WHO SAID THAT?

Your friend, John, has hurt his arm playing football and is taken to the hospital. Match the speakers and the pictures.

'John may have fractured his humerus. Nurse, arrange for him to go to X-ray please and I'll see him again as soon as the X-rays are ready.'
   Said by

'My arm hurts like anything. I'm bound to get it in the neck from Dad too. He said that I wasn't to play until after the exams and of course, it's got to be my right arm. Better try and see Mum first. She'll be OK.'
   Said by

'John Jenkins? You've got to have your picture taken. Let me help you on to the trolley and we'll be on our way. No this won't hurt. You're the third I've taken to X-ray this afternoon.'
   Said by

'Now that your arm has been set, you'll soon feel more comfortable. Remember what Doctor said. Take it easy and come back in three weeks. You'll need to go to reception to make an appointment.'
   Said by

'I wish I hadn't asked him to play. It wasn't a really important match, not like next week against the Green Devils. I suppose he'll be out of the team for months. I'll have to ask George to play centre forward. He'll be annoyed because I left him out today. I'm hungry too. I wish he'd hurry up.
   Thought by

STORY CARD

Give this picture a title then write a story about it. Check your sentence structure, paragraphing, punctuation and spelling.

Name _____

WORD FAMILIES

Find twelve word families. The first one has been found for you.

climb	take	climbing	climber	bought
walking	leavings	buyer	typist	typed
lightest	satisfies	types	walker	fighting
fought	teaching	fighter	explained	explaining
typing	takes	lights	left	lighter
buy	leaves	walked	teacher	walk
catching	teaches	lit	takings	climbed
explain	satisfy	fights	taught	leave
buying	took	walks	satisfied	type
catch	explains	buys	leaver	caught
fight	catcher	catches	taken	climbs
teach	light	satisfying	explanation	satisfaction

climb	climbing	climber	climbs	climbed

Name _____

TENSES

1. Underline verbs in the present tense, draw a circle around verbs in the past tense and draw a square around verbs in the future tense.

I enjoyed the ice cream.	John chased the dog.
I am helping Dad paint the garage.	The baby is crying.
I shall be ten next week.	We shall be on holiday next week.
It was a super film.	It rained all day yesterday.
The cat is going to have kittens soon.	This is my favourite T-shirt.

2. Underline all the verbs in the following passage on endangered species and then write it out in the past tense.

ENDANGERED SPECIES

Human beings are threatening the survival of many sea creatures. Some species are endangered: they survive in such small numbers that there is a real risk that they may die out altogether. But people continue to destroy them. The blue whale up to 30 metres long, is the largest known animal. It is harmless but like other whales is killed for its blubber and oil. Some animals starve because people kill or pollute their food. Some like seals are weakened by pollution so that they catch diseases and die. Modern fishing methods mean very large catches and fish populations become dangerously low. Humans destroy breeding grounds by dumping waste and poisons in the sea and by turning beaches into holiday resorts.

The Blue Whale

3. Write five suggestions that might help endangered species survive in the future. Make a draft of your answer and then make a fair copy.

4. The two reports below are about a race between tea clippers in 1866. The times for the journey were never bettered. Use the reports to write an account of the race in the past tense.

FOOCHOW, May 30, 1866

Fast and beautiful, tea clippers race along the route from Foochow in China to London, a distance of 16,000 miles. There is a bonus of £100 for the first captain home and 10s a ton extra on his tea cargo. 'Ariel,' 'Taeping' amd 'Serica' set sail today on the same tide from Foochow.

LONDON, September 6, 1866

After 99 days at sea, three tea clippers reach the Thames on the same tide and dock within two hours of each other. Packed with chests of the year's first tea crop, these fine sailing ships set a record that is going to be very difficult to beat.

A Tea Clipper

Name _____

THE OLD WOMAN AND THE PHYSICIAN

Read this draft adapted from the fable by Aesop, then write out your corrected version. Check capital letters, punctuation and spelling.

a ole woman having lost the us of here eyes, called in a fysician to heel them and made this bargin wiv him in the presense of witnesses. if he shoud cure her blindness, he shoud recieve from her a some of mony. if her ilness was not cured, she shoud giv him nothink. this agrement bein made, the fysician aplied creem to her eyes. on evry visit he took somethink belongin to her away untill he had stollen al her property. when he had stollen everythink he heeled her and demanded the promissed payment. the ole women when she had recovered her site saw that al her things had disapeared. she refused to pay him. the fysician took her too cort to get his mony. the ole woman agred that she had promised too pay the fysician if he cured her. 'he says i am cured but i canot see any of my posesions in my hous an so i must still be blind' she said.

1. How did the doctor try to cheat the lady in this story?

2. Is the lady in this story clever or stupid? Give reasons for your answer.

3. Draw a picture to illustrate this story.

Name _____

PREFIXES AND SUFFIXES

1. Add prefixes to these words and change their meanings.

   _____bid   _____do   _____take   _____day   _____vice

   _____chief   _____part   _____form   _____turn   _____vision

   Choose from   for-,   mis-,   un-,   tele-,   de-,   re-,   to-,   uni-.

2. Add prefixes to some of the words to change the meaning of what the policeman said.

   The policeman said, 'You are thoroughly __reliable and everything you do is

   __correct. I __trust you and __ agree with you. The work is __wanted.

3. Write complete sentences for each of the following words. The sentences should show their meanings.

   Import/export   encourage/discourage   appear/disappear

4. Add suffixes to change these words into adjectives

   sleep_____   digest_____   prefer_____   hope_____   ghost_____

   child_____   insist _____   house _____   angel _____   station _____

   Choose from   -ary,   -ing,   -ic,   -ish,   -ent,   -less,   -bound
                 -ible,   -ly,   -able

5. Add suffixes to change these words into nouns.

   Royal, young, perform, equip, congratulate, warm, waste, remove, employ, suggest.

6. Fill in the spaces with appropriate suffixes.

   We go to church to wor_____ . The church go_____pray quiet_____or sing hymns

   cheer_____ . There is usual_____an interest_____ sermon. After_____ we

   meet in the vestry. Once a year there is an annu_____ fete out_____ in the

   church grounds. The vicar directs proceed _____ using a mega_____ . People

   bring all kinds of glass_____ , cook_____ good_____ and homemade gifts.

   Choose from   -ware,   -ly,   -wards,   -ers,   -ed,   -ing/s,   -phone,
                 - fully,   -al,   -ship,   -side,   -ies.

Name

HANDWRITING

Practise your handwriting.

nut bin late sea time

hill ball milk add bad

man beach adder match

toast home log ready

field fun two time

woman name yes jelly

TEACHERS' NOTES AND RESOURCES

A wide variety of English skills is expected in the National Curriculum at Key Stage 2. Two of the most important are **speaking and listening.** The emphasis here is on the use of the spoken word as used in everyday conversation and in a number of speaking and listening situations. Children are expected to be able to convey a simple message, give and receive instructions accurately, respond to questions, take part in group discussions, use language to convey ideas and information, give a well organised and sustained account of an event, contribute to the planning of and participate in a group presentation and to recognise variations in language in regions and in social groups, that is, dialect and register.

Reading skills are an important part of the curriculum. It is essential to develop the ability to read, understand and respond to all types of writing. Information and retrieval skills are needed if the pupil is to proceed further up the educational ladder. Silent reading and oral skills are necessary as is an ability to express oneself fluently. Non-literary and literary texts are important in this development process.

Writing skills have to be developed. Pupils are expected to learn to construct and convey meaning in this work. They have to be able to produce written material using complete sentences, to produce chronological and non-chronological work and to write first, simple stories and then more complex ones with a proper structure. There is stress on the importance of well written and constructed stories, more developed sentence structure and an awareness of grammar and language. Later work requires more sophistication with pupils using a variety of forms for different purposes and audiences, handling sentence punctuation and direct speech, assembling their ideas on paper and recognising vocabulary and language variations.

Correct **spelling** is an important part of this written work. Regular polysyllabic words and regular patterns of vowel sounds should be recognised and pupils should show a growing awareness of word families and their relationships. Pupils should be able to check spelling accuracy when re-reading and revising their work. The proper use of prefixes and suffixes is an important part of this spelling work.

Handwriting is also considered and pupils should be able to begin to produce clear and legible joined-up writing in their own work.

Finally, there is **presentation.** This is consolidation of earlier work and pupils should by this time be able to spell complex words correctly, be able to check their writing for spelling errors and other errors of presentation and be able to produce clear and legible handwriting in printed and cursive styles.

The elements dealt with in this book are listed on the next page.

NATIONAL CURRICULUM ENGLISH LANGUAGE SKILLS KS 2

SPEAKING AND LISTENING SKILLS

Stories
Messages
Commenting
Giving instructions
Purposeful speaking
Questions and answers
Co-operation and presentation
Sustained reporting
Discussion
Language for information
Group presentation
Dialect and register

READING SKILLS

Reading aloud
Silent reading
Story line - settings, characters, main details
Characterisation
Story structure
Using the library
Reading with expression
Personal responses
Inference and prediction capabilities
Using catalogue systems
Explaining preferences
Critical skill development
Differences between fact and opinion
Finding out information for themselves
Awareness of the different uses of language

WRITING SKILLS

Use of complete sentences
Shaping writing chronologically
Writing more complex stories
Use of descriptive (non-chronological) writing
Revising and redrafting work
Proper use of punctuation
More sophisticated composition
Organise non-chronological writing for various purposes
Knowing how to use the structures of English properly
Writing in a variety of forms for different purposes
Proper use of organisational devices - sentences, punctuation, direct and indirect speech
Using standard and non-standard English properly
Ability to assemble ideas on paper and in discussion
Recognise vocabulary variations and use them appropriately.

SPELLING SKILLS

Spell correctly using common patterns
Recognise and use regular patterns for vowel sounds and common letter strings
Have an awareness of word families and their relationships
Ability to check their own spelling
Be able to use prefixes and suffixes correctly

HANDWRITING SKILLS

Be able to produce clear, legible, joined-up writing
Produce fluent joined-up writing in independent work

PRESENTATION SKILLS

Spell difficult words in their own work
Check final drafts of writing for errors in presentation and spelling
Produce clear and legible handwriting in printed and cursive styles

The notes which follow are designed to help teachers with strategies for teaching the skills in this very detailed syllabus. Inevitably, they cannot be completely comprehensive but we hope they will be useful in the classroom situation.

SPEAKING AND LISTENING SKILLS

FACTORS IN LISTENING, ANALYSING AND RE-TELLING

Stories include an analysis of Beginnings/Endings, Main Characters, Location/Situation and Mood or Atmosphere.

BEGINNINGS

Once upon a time . . .
Today, just before breakfast . . .
Later this month . . .
On Thursday, I am going to start . . .
Last week the snow began to fall . . .
I dislike my cousin Jane because . . .
My father was brought up in . . .

ENDINGS

I woke up with a jump. I had been dreaming.
Suddenly, it all ended as the vehicle came to an abrupt stop.
And the last thing we noticed was the limp of his left leg as he walked away.
The journey was over and he was so tired that he went upstairs.
Finally, he hurled back an insult and shook his fist at me.

MAIN CHARACTERS

Ask the children to say which are the main characters in a story. They should know who or what they are and why they are important to the story. How are the characters introduced?

LOCATION/SITUATION

Location and situation are also important and you can explain how these set the scene in a story. For example, it happened in the classroom, in the supermarket, by the river, at the youth club, in the tennis court, at dusk, at midnight, in the morning and so on.

MOOD/ATMOSPHERE

Is the story happy, sad, amusing, exciting, mysterious, fearful etc?
Consider the sentence
'The village clock chimed languidly in the hot midday sun . . .'
Village - this sets the place, the location.
midday - sets the time.
hot sun - tells us something about the day.
languidly - this helps set the mood or atmosphere, suggesting sleepiness or drowsiness.

Think of ploys to keep the children's interest.
1. Let them tell a story in their own words.
2. Let them re-tell a familiar story.
3. Let them re-tell a familiar story changing the beginning, the middle or the end.
4. Choose a very short story and tell it to the first child. He or she then whispers the story to the next child and so on. See how the story has changed after it has been passed on to several children or for a preset time. The last child tells the story as he or she heard it to the class.
5. Divide the class into groups giving each group a part of the story to act - the beginning, the middle or the end.
6. Use dolls or puppets so that the children can talk through them.
7. Use playing cards and divide the class into four groups.
   King and Queen - royalty
   Jack of clubs - knave, the villain
   Other jacks - three good men
   Other cards - ordinary people.
   The children tell a story using the cards.
8. Make a set of picture cards showing people involved in some activity or an event. Divide the children into groups, each group taking the beginning, middle or end of a story using the illustrations. Let them suggest possible beginnings and endings. Shuffle the cards and let the children start again.
9. Divide the class into two large groups. Each group should be given or should think of a story and draw their story for the other group to see. Let each group devise and tell the story.
10. Write a number of simple, well known rhymes and hymns or poems and divide them into beginnings, middles and endings. Use four children for each and ask them to arrange the parts in the correct order.

CONVEYING SIMPLE MESSAGES

There are numerous strategies to help children with taking and passing on messages.
1. Divide the class into two groups. Give one group a message to tell the other group. The message should be purposeful so that the children in the second group have to carry out a task.
2. Use hand radios or telephone (toy ones or old discarded ones). Give one group/s messages to pass to the other group/s.
3. Play 'Police-Call'. Allow the children to be police and villains, the former giving a message to track down and capture the baddies.
4. Allow the children to listen to any emergency call service and then ask them to pretend they are the service.
5. Play Chinese Whispers and let the children discover how messages change.
6. Make up messages for the children to speak. After this they should be able to make up their own and

SPEAKING AND LISTENING

the responses.
7. Let the class pretend to run a café and let the children order a meal. The messages have to be passed to the 'chef' and the meal served.
8. Running a post office offers further opportunities - buying stamps, postal orders, queries about forms . .
9. Pretend to be one of the emergency services - police, fire-brigade, ambulance, coast guard, AA, RAC . . . Begin by suggesting the message and response then let the class make up their own.
10. Other situations

    A newspaper reporter with a special story.

    A broadcaster with an SOS message.

    A television announcer with an important warning (river rising, flooding likely, severe weather) or story.

    A taxicab driver in touch with headquarters.

    A station announcer giving information about delays, arrivals and departures of trains.

    Airtraffic announcer giving information about delays, arrivals and departures of planes.

    A channel ferry or tunnel announcer.

    Coast guard giving details of an emergency situation and the organised rescue efforts.

Similarly, strategies can be adopted to help children convey messages to other children not in the same class, to adult teachers and to parents. Using a large scale map of the area around the school, children can be asked to tell a classmate how to get to a particular place on the map. This can be put into practice but children outside the school should be accompanied by staff.

LISTENING AND COMMENTING

There are a number of strategies to help pupils listen for longer periods of time. At first, tell the children what they are going to hear and if possible, what to concentrate on.
1. Use a tape recorder. Record the students speaking and let them listen to their own voices.
2. Record (a) prose and (b) poetry and ask the pupils to listen to these. A simple story is suitable for (a) and a poem such as 'Tiger, Tiger Burning Bright' would be suitable for (b).
3. Record music. It is more interesting if some information about the composer is given to the class before the music is played back. This may also encourage children to listen to more music.
4. The lyrics of modern 'pop' tapes/CDs are often interesting. Listening to the words spoken without the music and then as part of the song can start an interesting discussion. Remember to use short pieces of music.
5. Use a videotape to record a short documentary or nature programme for discussion.

All these listening activities can lead to discussion. Question and answer sessions are an important way of helping children to listen, speak and think for themselves. If the pupils are sufficiently advanced, one of them may pretend to be 'teacher' for part of the session.

FOLLOWING AND LEADING

The purpose of this section is to enable pupils to give instructions to others and also to carry out instructions themselves.

TASKS WITHIN A GROUP

Divide the class into groups and give the first group responsibilty for one task such as cleaning the blackboard while another group has to check that the chalk is ready for the teacher, another to water the flowers in the classroom and so on. The groups should be instructed verbally and after one week change jobs. The groups pass on the instructions to each other.

FURTHER TASKS WITHIN THE CLASSROOM

Further tasks include visual aid monitors, looking after equipment, caring for class pets, plants, temperature records . . . Pupils should be told exactly what has to be done. After a week, groups change their tasks and pass on their instructions. Children generally like responsibility providing it is within their capabilities and does not cause stress. Ensure that everyone has a share and that their efforts are noticed.

Other tasks within the classroom might be

The planning of a class project - this would be a combined effort with everyone contributing.

The planning of a storyline on the activities they took part in in a particular month or term.

A class wall display or chart. This could have a topic web and a large picture. Make sure the pupils plan what is to appear on the display or chart and make them keep to the plan.

TASKS OUTSIDE THE CLASSROOM

Pupils often find the task of organising something for the whole school a rewarding experience. Again, it should not be too ambitious and within the capabilities of the students. Contributing to morning assembly is often a good beginning. Several classes may work together on a theme such as 'The World Around Us,' 'Foreign Lands,' 'Looking after Pets,' or 'Travelling.' A more ambitious plan would be the organising of a religious service for the whole school, a reading and musical event, a concert, a pantomime or play.

Other planning tasks outside the classroom could be

Planning an outing or trip.

Planning a visit to a museum or local historical site.

Planning a visit to a neighbouring school.

Planning a Sports Day or a Sports Meeting.

In every case, the projects should be discussed verbally, instructions should be spoken not written and the pupils' efforts carefully monitored. A good idea is to have the pupils report back regularly, on how far they have progressed and when they expect to finish the task/s.

DETAILED ORAL ACCOUNTS

The pupils can choose from a variety of subjects and topics and from any part of the curriculum. Some ideas may be
1. A mathematical subject.
2. A scientific investigation.
3. A geographical survey.
4. An historical account.

SPEAKING AND LISTENING

5. A particular topic such as the school, the village or town where the children live, collecting stamps, collecting coins or a nature study.
6. A sporting event.
7. An imaginary account of a situation or an event.
8. Subjects from local history.

It is helpful to suggest how they should start and to discuss what they intend to cover in their account. Their talk can be illustrated with pictures, photographs, equipment (if relevant) or by demonstrating a skill.

The pupils may want to collaborate in their work preferring one of the group to do the actual talking. They may prefer to talk to the teacher alone or in a small group. Eventually the whole school might participate.

QUESTIONS AND ANSWERS

The purpose of this work is to give pupils an opportunity to ask and respond to questions. Designing an object offers opportunities for asking for information and providing answers to questions. Children can be divided into advisers and designers. Suitable projects might be

1. Design a suitable multi-purpose writing tool.
2. Design a suitable piece of class furniture, e.g. a desk.
3. Design a classroom.
4. Design the best layout for a school.
5. Design a layout for a football, cricket, or hockey pitch.
6. Design a layout for PE work.
6. Design a children's play area.
7. Design a children's garden.
8. Design a school uniform.
9. Design a school badge.
10. Design a board game.
11. Design a school programme of events.
12. Design a school newspaper.
13. Design a school concert.
14. Design a useful piece of classroom or PE equipment.
15. Design a school brochure.
16. Design an advertisement.

The children may need guidance in asking their questions.

Interviewing is more formal and it is helpful for the class to listen to interviews. There are plenty such as 'Desert Island Discs' on the radio and on the news programmes on the radio and on television as well as specialist chat shows. A tape recorder and video recorder help children to discuss how the interviews are put together, how the material is organised, how the interviewer controls the proceedings and how the questions are framed and in which order they are put. Pupils can be divided into groups and given lists of subjects. Examples include

1. Your family.
2. Your close relatives.
3. Your friends at home or at school.
4. Your main hobby or interest.
5. Your favourite radio/TV programme.
6. Your favourite pastime or sport.
7. Your culture.
8. Your religion.
9. Your village, town or city.
10. Your neighbourhood.
11. Your last holiday/Your next holiday.
12. A recent outing.
13. A real life event - a birthday, a wedding, a christening.
14. Traval by bus, train, ship or by air.
15. Something interesting that has happened to you such as getting lost, being left behind, the loss of some belongings.

Once the topics have been decided, the children should be divided into interviewers and interviewees. Six to ten questions are needed to begin with. Start with group interviews. The exercise can later be based on imaginary radio and TV interviews. 'Pop' stars and 'pop' music are useful starting points as are cartoon pictures. Recording the pupils' interviews helps them learn from the playbacks.

This question and answer situation can be adapted to role play and can be used extensively in games. Both these rely on questions asked with responses given. Real or imaginary role situations are fairly easy to devise.

Real situations can include a shop, post office, a bank, a travel agent, a coach station, a main line train station and an airport.

Situations involving questions include

1. Looking for lost property or a lost person.
2. Finding your way to a place.
3. Finding out how something works.
4. Detective questioning a suspect.
5. Doctor or nurse questioning a patient.
6. Police questioning a pedestrian or driver after an accident.
7. Fireman questioning someone who has been rescued.
8. Finding out what a relative wants for tea/dinner . . .
9. Finding out what other children do or play.
10. Making a shopping list.

The list is endless. Similarly, imaginary situations like asking a pet cat what it thinks about its home or asking a teapot how it likes being involved in tea-making can easily be devised.

An element of play is important in all Domino Master Files and the following are some of the many games that help with question and answer techniques.

1. A quiz. Typical question and answer game with an endless list of suitable topics.
2. Trivial pursuit. The board game can be adpated to suit the pupils.
3. Give me six. Write several interesting topics on the blackboard and pupils work in pairs to devise six questions about one of the topics.
4. What's my line? Pupils mime the actions of a character and the class can ask up to 20 questions and guess the name of the character - famous person or occupation.
5. Complicated questions. This aims to make the pupils puzzle over the answer. For example,
What is 'the greenhouse effect'?
Why does water boil?
6. Cartoon speech bubbles. Children have to decide what the cartoon characters are saying.

SPEAKING AND LISTENING

7. Piggy in the Middle. One pupil is 'it' and is asked questions about himself/herself. The child must not use the pronoun 'I' but can use his or her name.
8. 'Yes' or 'No' questions. Children are to answer questions without saying 'yes' or 'no' in their replies. Some become very good at this and it may be necessary to introduce a time limit.
9. Strange Object Game. Collect a number of 'old' unfamiliar objects for the class to look at. The class has 20 questions to find out what it is. Objects could include an old passport, a sugar caster, a pepper pot, a miner's lamp, a cigarette holder, a lighter, an old tin opener, a quill pen, an adjustable spanner, a spinning top, a bed warmer, a deed, a shoe horn.
10. Mastermind. Devise a series of questions for the children on a particular subject. Divide them into two groups, the questioners and those who answer. This can be extended by letting one group research questions and putting one child to answer. Different children are 'it' in subsequent games.
11. Call My Bluff. Give groups of 4 to 6 children a selection of unusual words with the correct definitions. They have to think of alternative plausible definitions for the words and the rest of the class have to decide the correct answer.
12. Pork Pies and Apple Tarts. A child thinks of an object which is then called the 'pork pie' or 'apple tart'. Working in small groups, the questioners try to find out what the object is. They use 'pork pie' or 'apple tart' in their questions, e.g.
How long is your pork pie?
Is your apple tart noisy?
Is your apple tart small or big?
What colour is your pork pie?

WORKING TOGETHER

Children can work together in a number of ways. They can write collectively, producing a piece of work to which all contribute. They can also plan an outing or activity or give personal views on particular subjects. Debates, trials (e.g. a court scene in which they all take part) are also types of group activities. They may work together to produce a story or report for a newspaper or television news programme.

PRESENTATIONS

Children usually love to act and are easily persuaded to play different roles. It is a good idea to start with familiar stories like *The Three Bears, Aladdin, The Wizard of Oz, Cinderella, Jack and the Beanstalk, Dick Whittington, Sleeping Beauty, Mother Goose, Snow White and the Seven Dwarfs, Rumpelstiltskin* and so on. Change the stories to add interest and follow these by real-life role situations such as a decorating task that went wrong, a minor kitchen accident, an argument in a shop or store or the search for a special gift.

SUSTAINED REPORTING

This is intended to give children practice in presenting an account of an event or activity from their own point of view such as a report of an event, describing an activity in which they took part or talking about something they like or dislike.

DISCUSSION

Children should be encouraged to discuss matters relevant to them in school and at home. TV or videos can help to get discussions under way.

LANGUAGE FOR INFORMATION

Children should also be encouraged to give an account of things they have seen at home or at school. To help them with this skill, place items on a tray and ask them to remember them. After a short time, remove the tray and either take some items away or replace one or two by different ones. Personal possessions can also be used in this activity and children can describe their most cherished possessions from memory.

GROUP PRESENTATIONS

The children can be given further practice in planning and presenting their work for the class. They need guidelines (roles, subject, audience, form, plan, props etc.) before they start. They can also do the same with stories.

DIALECT AND REGISTER

Most classes have children from different backgrounds - Scottish, Irish, Welsh and English dialects are the most obvious but there are children from other ethnic backgrounds - West Indies, Pakistan, India and so on. Make sure that regional accents such as Birmingham, Newcastle are also noted.

Record them on tape if possible so that they can be played back. Vocabulary differs too and regional words should be pinpointed and recorded. Social groups and occupations may differ and this may be reflected in the way they talk and the vocabulary they use - register.

READING SKILLS

PARTS OF A BOOK
Children need to be introduced to parts of a book, where they are in a book and what is to be found in each.
1. The front cover.
2. The spine.
3. The back cover.
4. Inside the book - Introduction and Foreword.
6. Contents page.
6. The pages themselves.
7. Illustrations.
8. The beginning, the middle and the end.
9. Index.
10. How a book is made.

READING ALOUD
Children should practice reading aloud. Drama and poetry are excellent vehicles for development of this skill. Children need help with
1. The volume of their voices.
2. The pitch of their voices.
3. Making pauses at dramatic points.
4. Speeding up a little when the action requires it.
5. Slowing down when the action requires it.
6. Raising or lowering their voices to dramatise events or speech.
7. Developing a repertoire of voices for different characters in a story.

Many occasions may be used for this type of reading including taking part in the school assembly, reading passages from scriptures and saying prayers.

SILENT READING
This should be encouraged by having a separate part of the classroom set aside for this (a reading corner), by having a definite time for reading, a good supply of suitable books and reading material. The school library is an extension of this.

STORY ANALYSIS
Reading stories is very important and children have to be encouraged to take part in story analysis. This includes
1. Storyline - humorous, sad, exciting or frightening.
2. Main details of the story. Is there a climax, a turning point, a surprise ending?
3. Sequence of events. A story map is useful to record these.
4. An analysis of characters. Contrasting and comparing characters. Are the characters good or bad, sad or funny or a combination of a number of qualities? Show that characters need not be human. They may be creatures from outer space, animals, monsters, witches or dragons and so on.
5. What the story is about.
6. The setting. When, where, the atmosphere (e.g a dark night, a sunny morning, at the seaside, in the country, in a deserted house, an empty room).
7. How the story unravels - the *denouément*.
8. Illustrations. These are particularly important in children's stories.
9. Predictions. How the story begins, develops and ends. (Encourage the children to guess how the story continues and finishes. If possible let them make up alternative endings.)
10. Style - descriptive, humorous, sad, exciting and so on.

Show how the ability of the writer keeps the reader interested throughout the story.

USING THE LIBRARY
At this stage of their learning, children should be able to find information in the class and school libraries. Explain that books are either fact or fiction. Fact involves information, and fiction is about stories that are not true. Children should be given a suitable subject dealing with facts to investigate. Be sure the information is available in the library. They have to decide whether they need to use books that are biographical, historical, geographical, scientific or mathematical or a combination of these.

TOPIC WEBS
Topic Webs are useful. The class may be given a wide topic to research. The topic can be divided into different sections and groups collect information on different parts. See the topic web for 'Light' on the next page.

This could be further extended by considering light as an adjective (airy, buoyant, delicate, flimsy, faint, gentle, soft, weak, small, thin, amusing, funny, humorous etc.) A good way of starting a topic web is with a Thesaurus.

USING CONTENTS AND INDEXES, ENCYCLOPAEDIAS AND OTHER MATERIAL
Most books of fact have a contents page at the beginning which is the guide to the information to be found within the book. Similarly, at the back of the book, there may be an index containing, in alphabetical order, fuller details of what is in the book. Encyclopaedias are useful for information and the letters on the spine give an indication of what is in each volume. The index, which may be a volume on its own, gives more detailed information about the location of information. Teaching children to use a dictionary, a thesaurus and an encyclopaedia gives them skills that will always be useful. The title and subtitle of a book indicates what it is about.. Games like 'Hunt the Book', 'Hunt the Title' or 'Follow that Alphabet' may be used.

READING

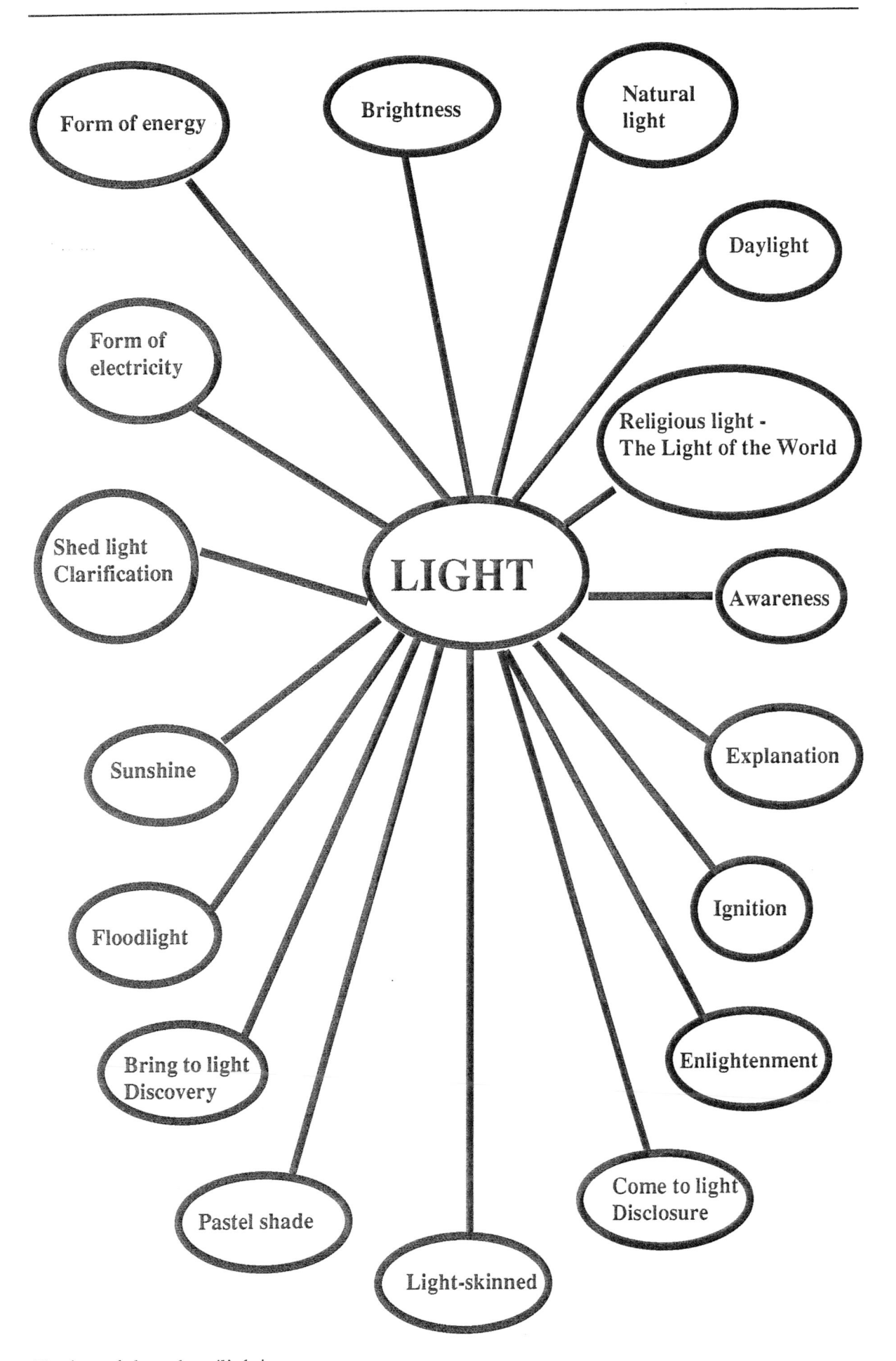

- Form of energy
- Brightness
- Natural light
- Daylight
- Form of electricity
- Religious light – The Light of the World
- Shed light / Clarification
- **LIGHT**
- Awareness
- Sunshine
- Explanation
- Floodlight
- Ignition
- Bring to light / Discovery
- Enlightenment
- Pastel shade
- Come to light / Disclosure
- Light-skinned

Topic web based on 'light'.

READING WITH EXPRESSION

This is a skill to be learned. Children have to be taught to read to create mood, show emotion and to build a repertoire of voices. They need to be encouraged to give their personal responses to stories, other types of writing and poetry. They can be helped to predict events and storylines using inference and deduction and by using prediction exercises and cloze tests.

CATALOGUING SYSTEMS

To complete the information on using a library, children should be introduced to the various cataloguing systems. These include alphabetical indexes of books by authors, the use of computers for storage and retrieval and the most widely used system of classification, the Dewey Decimal Classification. This divides factual, non-fiction books into ten main groups represented by figures on the spines of the books.

SCANNING AND SKIMMING

It is at this stage that children need to be introduced to the levels of reading known as scanning and skimming. Scanning is glancing quickly over a text looking for specific items or references of information. Skimming is reading quickly so as to obtain the general gist of a passage or to locate a particular section in a book.

ANALYTICAL AND CRITICAL DEVELOPMENT

Children now have to consider their personal views on material they have read. They should have become more analytical. They need to be aware of the nature of the subject matter, how it has been presented, the characters, the plot, the style, what language has been used, the readability of the material, illustrations used and the combination of features which held their interest until the book/story finished. More than this, they should be able to say why they like a particular piece. This is the time for them to listen to critical comment on the radio or TV and read elementary reviews in newspapers and magazines. Children should be encouraged to write their own reviews.

To improve their critical powers, children need to be provided with a variety of material such as

- Stories - these may be factual, true or untrue, real or imaginary
- Non-fiction
- Instructional material
- Poetry - rhyming, blank verse, modern poetry
- Magazines
- Comics
- Advertising material
- Letters/speeches
- Posters
- Visual aids of all types

Straightforward comparisons of different articles on the same subject, different slants on topical stories, different emphasis in speeches by different people, different approaches in advertising are all relevant here.

FACT AND FICTION

We are bombarded by so much information in so many ways that an analytical approach is essential to distinguish fact from fiction, the possible from the highly unlikely. Children need to be aware of the differences between solid fact and opinion and the more perceptive child should be able to recognise bias.

THE USE OF LANGUAGE

Children should also become more aware of the ways in which language is being used. Humour, the use of colourful words, imagery, (especially metaphor) and the use of dialogue are all part of this work. They should be able to analyse advertisements, at least at an elementary level, in newspapers, magazines, on hoardings, on the radio, on the television and elsewhere.

WRITING SKILLS

ILLUSTRATIONS
To begin with, plenty of illustrations are needed so that the words and pictures appear together. Simple sentences to complete using pictures are introduced at this stage. It is important for the children to write in complete sentences. Distinguish between phrases and sentences.

PARTS OF SPEECH
Introduce nouns (naming words) and verbs (doing words) explaining how the latter are the most important in sentence construction. Cards or worksheets are useful so that children can pinpoint nouns and verbs. Distinguish between common and proper nouns.

SEQUENCING
It is a good idea to use nouns and verbs in sequencing exercises and you can lead into this using pictures in the wrong order. The children cut out the pictures and paste them up in the correct order. They can then write the sequences out using the pictures. Sorting sentences and putting them in order is also useful and as children learn to join sequences with conjunctions like 'and' and 'but' they can start to use more complex structures and different joining words.

DESCRIPTIVE WORK
More complex stories can now be introduced and children can attempt descriptive work. The descriptions of characters, their feelings and behaviour are important. To aid descriptions, pupils should now be introduced to adjectives, describing words, and simple adverbs. Different settings and locations for stories can be considered. It becomes possible for the students to predict the ending of a story and to suggest alternatives for such endings.

NON-CHRONOLOGICAL WRITING
Non-chronological writing could now follow on from the stories. This could begin with the children describing a simple object in front of them. They should be able to touch it and feel it. If it is not too heavy or fragile, they should pick it up and examine it in their hands. A plan of campaign for such descriptions is useful.

Name the object.
What it is.
What it is used for.
Describe its properties - structure, shape, size, weight, colour, general appearance.
Name separate parts if any and describe them.
Compare the object with others that are similar.

WRITING PLANS
Plans are helpful when describing people or places.

People
Name, age, sex, living or dead.
Physical characteristics - height (tall, short, medium), build (thin, heavy, fat, bony), hair (long, short, straight, curly, balding, colour), colour of eyes and skin, distinguishing marks if any.
Personal characteristics (like stutter, squint etc.)
The way the person walks.
Dress - clothes, how they are worn, spectacles or not.
Character and personality - happy, sad, morose, shy, withdrawn, aggressive, talkative, introvert, extrovert and so on.

Places
General remarks about the place, position and size of the location.
Precise features - vegetation, buildings, roads, railways etc.
When being described - time of day, weather...
Colour and shapes are important.
Exteriors/interiors of buildings.
Compare and contrast the place with other similar ones.
Points of special interest.
Anything that makes it memorable or important.

REVISING AND REDRAFTING
Finally, it is important that children learn to read their work over, revising and redrafting. It is a good idea to have children write first on rough paper or better, keep an exercise book for rough work. Then discuss what they think is good about the work. They need to be encouraged and improvements should be commended. Correcting all the errors may destroy a child's confidence. It may be best to concentrate on the purpose of the exercise and keep other corrections to a minimum. To correct or not to correct is always a matter of judgement, especially when new and perhaps difficult material is introduced. A child can only learn so much at a time. If the work is appropriate to the child's ability and development, this should not be a problem. It is helpful if the work is conceived as a joint activity, a combined activity, the purpose of which is accurate, well-written work.

LAYOUT AND PUNCTUATION
Layout and punctuation are important. Pupils should know that capital letters start sentences, are used for initials, for abbreviations and for acronyms (e.g. B.B.C., A.A., R.A.C.) Students should now be introduced to paragraphs and punctuation.

The general rule for paragraphs is that each deals with one main idea or topic (one topic = one paragraph). The first sentence usually indicates what a paragraph is about and is called the topic sentence. Children should be given a selection of topic sentences and asked to write a

WRITING

paragraph on each. Four or five sentences are expected. Examples of topic sentences are

I like growing things.
We live near a bird sanctuary.
We have a dog/cat ... called ...
My home town, ... is near ...
I recently saw the film ...
I dislike beef burgers/unexpected visitors ...

Material for topic paragraphs can be found in books, comics, magazines, newspapers ...

Full stops, question marks, exclamation marks, commas and punctuation for direct speech should all be dealt with now. Other uses of inverted commas - for foreign words, slang words, local words and specialist words are the most obvious as well as around titles of books, newspapers, magazines, films, plays, TV and radio programmes, songs and commercial product names.

COMPOSITION MATERIAL

Composition material and exercises are legion and the Pupils' Worksheets suggest a variety of work. Below are a few ideas to encourage children to write.

1. Unusual and interesting objects - old and new can be brought to school and used for descriptive work. (E.g. an old iron, an old £5 note, old pottery, an old sword, a flintlock pistol, a map, a candlestick, a candle, a candle-snuffer, a lovespoon, an apostle spoon, a wooden clothes peg, a corn dolly, a ring, a beach pebble, an egg timer.)
2. Photographs of people, individuals, famous people, relatives, school groups, shots of places - villages, towns, cities, railways, airports, hospitals.
3. Historical snapshots or historical pictures of people and places as 'they used to be'. Photographs showing rooms with 'old' furniture in them such as kitchens, bedrooms and parlours. Comparisons between yesterday and today usually evoke plenty of interest and comment. Photographs of what used to be fashionable clothes - not necessarily very long ago.
4. Ask the children to talk to grandparents about what it was like when the grandparents were children. Compare childhood then and now.
5. Pictures and stories that children cut from old magazines and newspapers.
6. TV programmes. Accounts can be descriptive but children usually have strong opinions about these too.
7. Watching documentaries as a class provides interesting material.
8. An account of an unusual adventure or happening at home, on holidays or in school.
9. Encourage visitors to school to tell about their work or experiences.
10. School visits to museums, zoos, suitable businesses, works etc.
11. Pets make interesting subjects and the biology teacher may have some that can be used as topics - especially by those children who do not have their own.

Organisational devices help such as
story boards,
story maps,
relationship diagrams,
sequencing and
prediction ploys.

Further non-chronological writing has to be taught and here the emphasis should be on planning before the children start to write. This includes work on a subject they enjoy, writing a guide book for a stranger to the area, personal and business letters, invitations and they should also have practice in composing rhymes and poetry. Limericks and jokes are also a source of fun in written work.

ELEMENTARY ANALYSIS

The more complicated structures of English can be considered now. These include analysis of a simple sentence into subject and predicate, the types of phrases (adjectival, adverbial and noun) and the division of complex sentences into main clause and subordinate clauses.

WRITING FOR SPECIFIC PURPOSES

Children should be told that written work for different purposes takes different forms. Writing for particular purposes is the key and this includes letters, plans, instructions, messages, posters, diaries and stories. Imaginative writing is also most important and in all cases planning the work is essential. The children must know the writing purpose (for whom the written work is intended), the ability and interests of the recipient, whether illustrations are needed and the kind of format. Organisational devices are useful in helping children understand this work. It is necessary to divide written work into standard English - formal language and style and non-standard English (poems, stories with colloquial language, radio programmes and drama).

REGISTER

Finally, the children should be introduced to the different registers of English. They should understand that there are numerous forms of specialist knowledge and therefore specialist English vocabulary, e.g. the scientist, pharmacist, doctor, baker, butcher, printer, antique dealer, mechanic and many more have their own terminology. Collect specialist language from books and magazines so that the pupils learn to recognise the different forms. The children can then write pieces using variations of register.

SPELLING SKILLS

LOOK, COVER, WRITE AND CHECK

The ability to spell is related closely to phonic letter understanding and a memory for words. The names and sounds of the 26 letters of the alphabet should be taught and they should know the long and short vowels,

a e i o u

and that 'y' can sometimes be used as a vowel as in words like 'sky' and 'my'.

All children should be taught the **look, cover, write and check** method of learning to spell. It is important to remember that there are high frequency words - those words which are irregular but are used 50% of the time.

HIGH FREQUENCY WORDS

about	dinner	home	nothing	some
and	do	horse	now	street
all	doll	house	no	table
another	door	how	of	take
any	down	into	off	tea
are	eat	keep	once	tell
apple	egg	know	one	these
away	every	last	only	they
back	fast	letter	open	think
ball	father	like	other	three
because	fell	little	our	time
be	find	live	over	to
been	first	look	own	today
before	five	made	picture	too
bird	fly	make	place	toy
black	for	many	play	train
blue	four	May	put	tree
book	found	Mr.	rabbit	under
boy	gave	Mrs.	road	very
brother	girl	me	read	walk
bush	give	milk	round	was
by	go	money	said	water
call	going	morning	saw	we
came	grandad	more	say	white
children	green	mother	school	why
could	have	my	sea	work
come	head	name	she	woman
cousin	her	new	should	would
cow	here	next	sister	year
day	hill	night	so	you

Also: January, February, March, April, May, June, July, August, September, October, November, December, one, two, three, four, five, six, seven, eight, nine, ten.

If these words are learnt then the general spelling of the class will improve. Using look, cover, write and check, the words can be learnt four or five at a time. Word games such as word squares, word grids, word completion exercises, sorting into sets, dictionary searches, lotto cards, pairing words, card spinners, word jumble exercises, crosswords, spelling B's and competitions help. Vowels and common letter strings can be learned in the same way. A tape recorder is often useful for this work. Children should be taught to look for relationships between words and to use them in context.

CHECKING SPELLING

It is important that children learn to check their own spellings. They should have access to a good dictionary and refer to it as often as possible. They should keep it by their side for constant reference so it will fix the meanings and spellings in their minds. They can also make their own spelling books and word banks. There are numerous word processors and spelling checkers on the market which can be used effectively.

PREFIXES AND SUFFIXES

The most common prefixes and suffixes should be taught. Students can look them up in a dictionary, make their own lists and discover how prefixes can be added to change the meanings of words. Give the children a list of prefixes and let them work out what they mean. The complex rules for suffixes should be avoided at this stage but they should be aware of how suffixes can change meanings.

Each child should have a list of the common prefixes in their exercise books and to start their lists they should look up the common prefixes and their meanings in their dictionaries. A list is given below to help with this work.

PREFIXES

Prefix	Meaning	Example
a-	on, out, up	askew
ab-, abs	away, from	absent
ad-	to, towards	adhesive
ambi-	on both sides	ambidextrous
an-, a-	not	anarchy
ante-	before	antecedent
anti-	against	antidote
arch-	chief	archangel
auto-	self	autobiography
bene-	well	benefit
bi-	twice, two	bifocal
bio-	life	biology
circum-	around	circumference
com-	with, together	comrade
con-	with, together	conform
contra-	against	contrary
counter-	against	counterfoil
de-	down, away	descent
demi-	half	demigod
dia-	through, across	diameter
dis-	not, away from, apart	disappear
em-/en-	in, on	envelope
epi-	upon, above	epicentre
equi-	equal	equidistant
ex-	out, forth, away	exhale
ex-	formerly, used to be	ex-skipper
extra-	outside, beyond	extraordinary
fore-	before, in front of	foreword
hemi-	half	hemisphere
hexa-	six	hexagon
homo-	same, similar	homogeneous
hyper-	over, above	hypercritical
hypo-	below, under	hypodermic
in-/il-/im-/ir-	not, in, on, into against, towards	inadequate impossible irrelevant
inter-	between, among	interval
intro-	inwards	introvert
mal-	ill, bad	malady
male-	evil	malevolent
met-/meta-	change	methodical metamorphosis
mis-	wrong, badly	mistake
mono-	one, single	monocle
non-	not	nonsense
ob-	against	object
oct-/octa/octo-	eight	octane October
omni-	all	omnipotent
out-	beyond	outcast
over-	too much, above	overcast
pan-	all, united	pantomime
penta-	five	pentagon
per-	through	perforate
peri-	around	perimeter
phil(o)-	love, loving	philology
poly-	many	polyglot
post-	after, behind	postpone
pre-	before	prevention
pro-	for, forward on behalf of	proceed
proto-	first	prototype
pseud(o)-	false	pseudonym
quad-	four	quadrilateral
re-	again, back, down	recede
retro-	back	retrospective
semi-	half	semicircle
sub-	under	submarine
super-	over, above	supercede
tele-	far, at a distance	telescope
trans-	across	transfer
tri-	three	tripod
ultra-	extreme	ultrasonic
un-	not, lack of	unlike
uni-	one	unicorn
under-	below, too little	undergraduate
vice-	in place of	vice-chairman
with-	against	withstand

SPELLING

SUFFIXES

Suffix	Example
-able, -ible, -ble	admirable, edible
-acious	audacious
-age	homage
-aholic	workaholic
-al,	comical, equal
-an, ane	urban, urbane,
-ance, -ancy, -ence, -ency	distance, cadence, decency
-ant,	assistant, arrogant
-arch, -archy	monarchy, hierarchy
-ate, -ee, -ey, -y	curate, committee, attorney, jury
-ate, -ete, -eet, -te, -ute, -te	deliberate, concrete, discreet, minute
-bound	housebound
-centric	concentric, eccentric
-cide	homicide, herbicide
-craft	aircraft, woodcraft
-cy	accuracy
-dom	boredom, kingdom
-ed	started, green-eyed
-ee	employee, matinée
eer	gazetteer, pioneer
-el, -le	shovel, brittle, chapel, mongrel
-en	chicken, wooden
-ence	dependence
-ent	persistent, student
-er	bigger, baker
-ery	cookery, crockery
-esce	effervesce
-ese	Chinese, Americanese
-esque	statuesque
-ess	actress, duchess
-est	biggest, youngest
-et, -ete,- ate	poet, athlete, apostate
-ette, -et	cigarette, pocket
-fold	twofold, manifold
-folk	townsfolk, kinsfolk
-free	carefree, duty-free
-friendly	user-friendly
-ful	bagful, awful
-gon	polygon, pentagon
-gram	diagram, telegram
-graph	autograph, photograph
-hand	farmhand, left-hand
-head	hothead, letterhead
-hood	childhood, priesthood

Suffix	Example
-ian	electrician,
-iana	Victoriana
-ible, -ibility	digestible/digestibility
-ic, -ical	angelic, philosophical
-ice, -ise	avarice, justice, exercise
-ics	electronics, physics
-id	placid, splendid
-ide	oxide, sulphide
-ie, -y	laddie, baby, doggy
-ify	beautify, simplify
-ile, -il, -eel, -le	fragile, genteel, frail, humble
-ine	canine, feline
-ing	running, jumping
-ion,-tion, -ition, -sion,	action, opinion, occasion, ransom
-som, -som	
-ise, -ize	baptise, criticise
(-ize is not always an acceptable alternative e.g. advise)	
-ish	biggish, Scottish
-ish	banish, punish
-isk	asterisk, obelisk
-ism	criticism, Thatcherism
-ist	idealist, botanist
-ite	unite
-ition	see -ion
-itis	arthritis, appendicitis
-ity	curiosity, personality
-ive,	fugitive, active
-ize	see -ise
-k	hark, stalk
-kin	lambkin
-less	fearless, ageless
-let	piglet, bracelet
-like, -ly	birdlike, orderly
-ling	duckling, darling
-ly	clearly, daily
-ma	asthma, diploma
-man	milkman, Englishman
-mate,	classmate
-ment	achievement
-meter	barometer, thermometer
-metre	kilometre, centimetre
-monger	fishmonger
-most	uppermost, foremost
-n	torn
-naut	cosmonaut, astronaut
-ness	sadness, witness

Suffix	Example
-nik	beatnik, refusenik
-ock	bullock, paddock
-ocracy	democracy, bureaucracy
-ocrat	democrat, bureauocrat
-oid	spheroid, tabloid
-ology	technology, archaeology
ological	biological
-or	collector, calculator
-ory	auditory, illusory
-osis	cirrhosis, osmosis
-our	honour, savour
-ous, -ose	famous, grandiose
-person	chairperson
-phile, philic	bibliophile, hydrophilic
-phobia	claustrophobia
-phone	telephone
-piece	showpiece
-proof	heatproof
-red	hatred, kindred
-ridden	class-ridden, disease-ridden
-scape	landscape
-ship	friendship
-side	bedside
-sis	analysis
-some	quarrelsome
-speak	'newspeak'
-ster	youngster
-stricken	poverty-stricken
-style	freestyle
-ther	hither
-tor	actor
-tude	altitude, fortitude
-ular	muscular
-und	rotund
-ure	closure, culture
-ward(s)	seaward, awkward
-ware	glassware, silverware
-wise, -ways	streetwise, sideways
-woman	horsewoman
-work	brasswork, shiftwork
-wright	shipwright
-y	moody, misery, Jimmy, Betty

HANDWRITING SKILLS

Children should be sitting comfortably at the table. Elbows and arms should rest on the table. All fingers, except the first, should be underneath the pencil. The free hand should hold the paper or exercise book firmly. Begin with patterns and then with letters that easily join at the bottom (base line joins).

aaa   ccc   eee

Then join these letters to make words, e.g.

boat

Next deal with letters joined at the top.

oror   vovo

Again put them in words.

world

The letter 'f' needs special consideration. It is joined at the crossbar in

forget

and so on. It is not joined to another 'f'.

At first, children's writing is too small and later it tends to be too large. With guidance they soon settle for an appropriate size.

Cross joins to oval letters are difficult for some children and they need to practise as often as possible. 'r' also can be difficult.

oa   od

With practice, children learn to join 'r' to any other letter.

Remember to tell the children to take their pencils off the paper after each of the following:

b, s, x, p, g, y, j and q.

It is a matter of individual preference whether these join at all. If a join is taught then the letters usually join from the bottom line.

The letters 'x' and 'z' are better not joined because they are hard to recognise in the middle of words.

Cross joins need plenty of practice, for example

woman

and joining descenders with hooks, for example

jump

At A4 level, they will find it more interesting to write out a short passage.

PRESENTATION SKILLS

It is important that children learn from the beginning to set good, realistic standards for themselves. They need to understand that it is necessary to appraise their own work. Learning to find their own errors and correct them is an invaluable skill.

Presentation involves the consolidation of all the work they have done. They need to check their spelling, grammar, sentence structure, paragraphing and the organisation of their work. Using a spell-checker or a word processor is not as sound as learning to use a dictionary. Clear, neat handwriting adds to the overall presentation.

STORYBOARD

TOPIC WEB

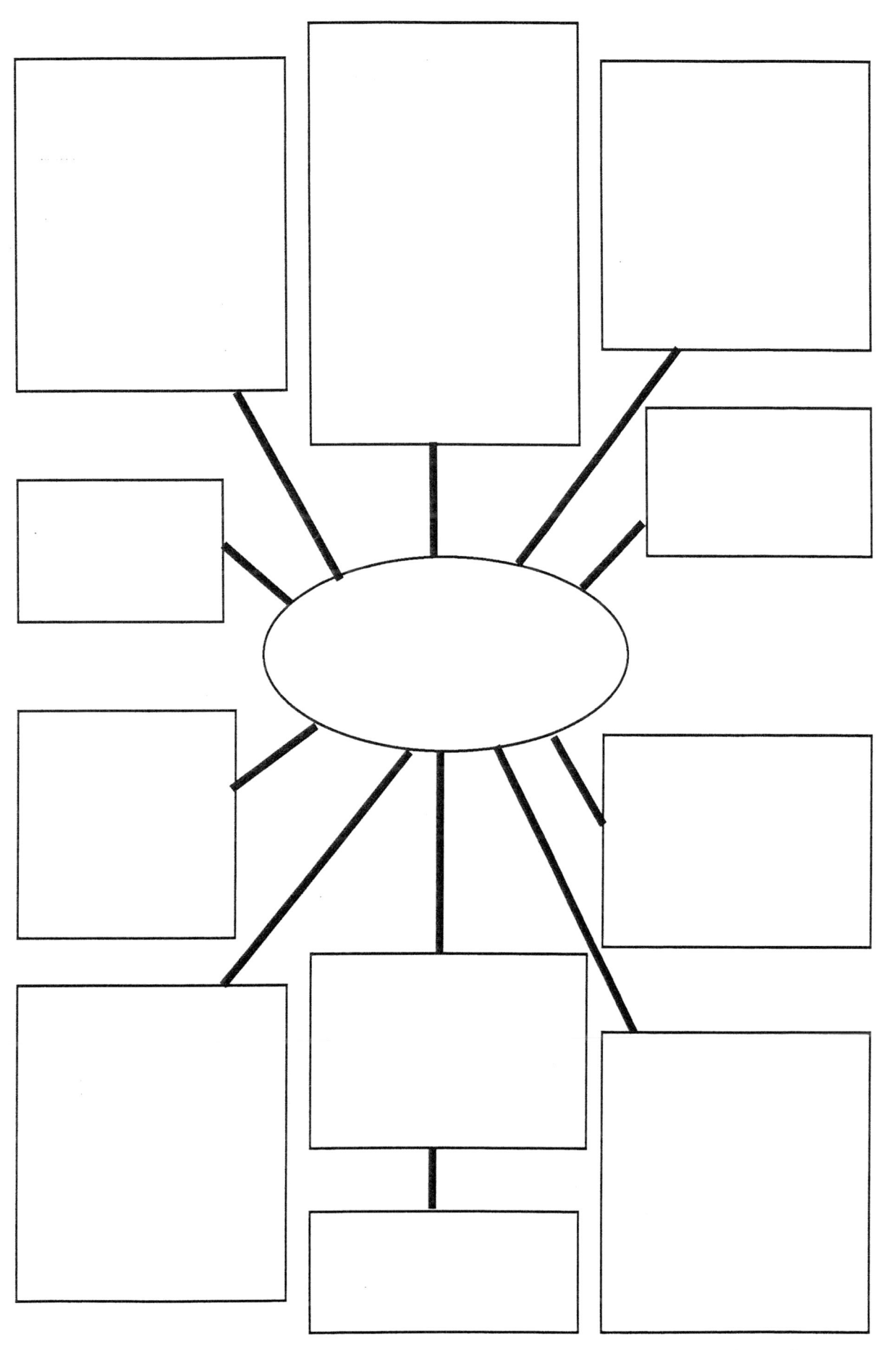

IDEAS WEB

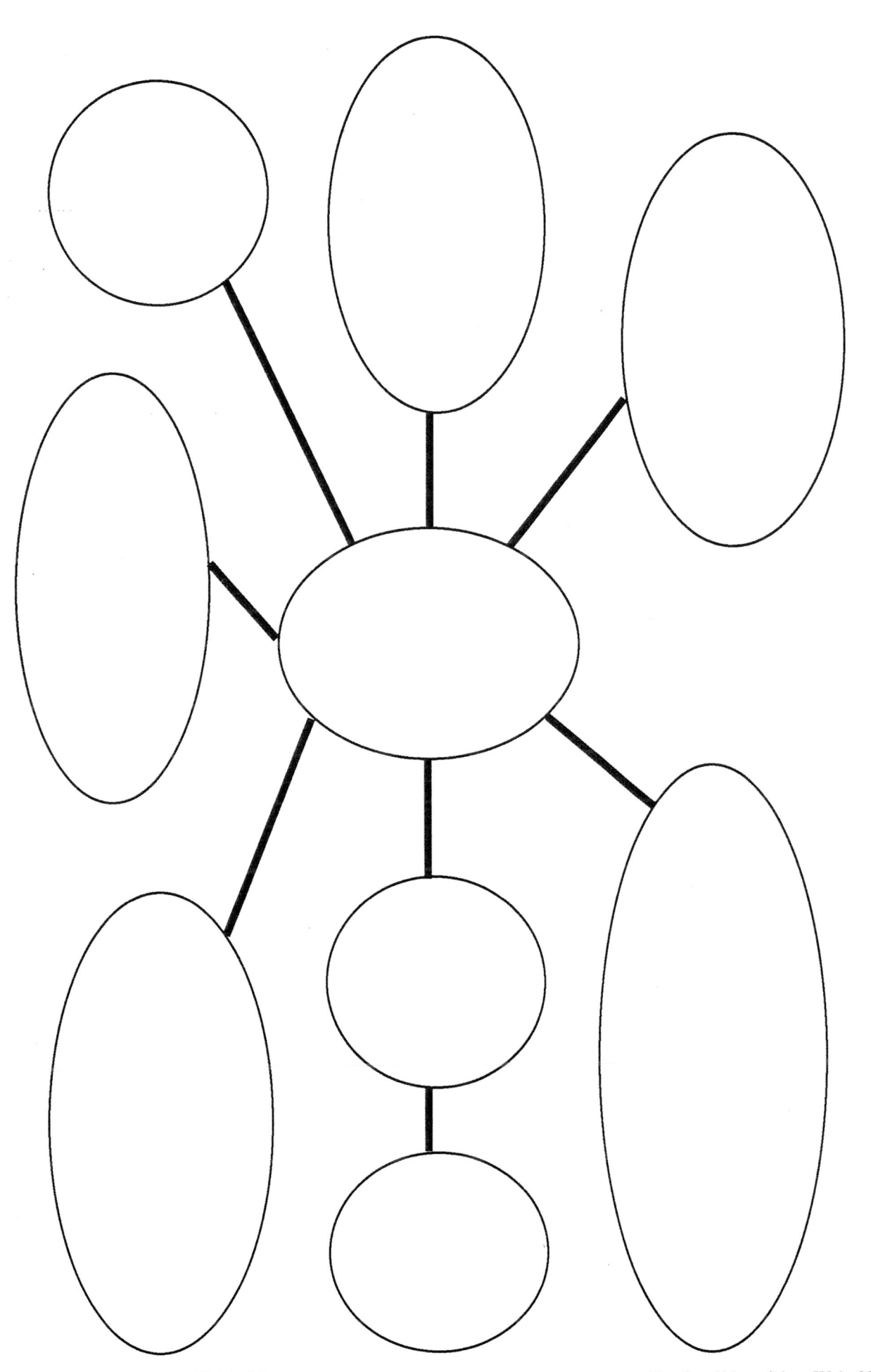

WRITING A LETTER
ADDRESSING AN ENVELOPE

WRITING PRACTICE

RECORD SHEET
ENGLISH KS2

Name _____ Age _____

Page	Master Copy		Page	Master Copy	
5	Speaking and Listening		42	What Happened Before?	
6	Storyboard		43	Missing Words	
7	What's Happened?		44	The Dewey System	
8	Messages		45	Where Can I Find It?	
9	Listening		46	In the Kitchen	
10	Planning a Visit		47	On The Farm	
11	Planning a Wall Display About Where I Live		48	Finding Out	
			49	In Hospital	
12	A Scientific Investigation		50	Bookshelf	
13	Be a Designer		51	Facts or Opinions?	
13	Gardening Club		52	Advertisements	
14	The Interview		53	Research Project 1	
15	Conservation		54	Research Project 2	
16	We Did This		55	The Right Word	
17	Bookings		56	The Crocodile	
18	I Do Not Like Camping!		57	The Big Rock Candy Mountains	
19	Save Our School		58	Sentences 1	
20	When My Brother (or Sister) was Born		59	Sentences 2	
			60	Nouns	
21	Lost and Found		61	Doing Words 1	
22	A News Programme		62	Doing Words 2	
23	Who Said It?		63	Information Sentences	
24	Story of the Week		64	Describing Words 1	
25	Character Study		65	Describing Words 2	
26	Putting a Story Together		66	Adverbs	
27	Story Detective 1		67	Questions 1	
28	Story Detective 2		68	Questions 2	
29	Story Detective 3		69	Punctuation	
30	What Happens Next?		70	Sentences 3	
31	Gelert and the Wolf		71	Layout	
32	Storyboard		72	Life in a Castle	
33	The Front Cover of a Book		73	The 'Royal George'	
34	The Spine of a Book		73	Four Things	
35	The Contents Page of a Book		74	Who Said That?	
36	The Index of a Book		75	Story Cards	
37	Using an Encyclopaedia		76	Word Families	
38	Different Voices		77	Tenses	
39	A Story or Poem I Have Enjoyed Reading		78	The Old Woman and the Physician	
			79	Prefixes and Suffixes	
40	Travelling by Train		80	Handwriting	
41	What Happens Next?				

English KS2 Master File © E J P & D C P

MASTER FILES

published by
Domino Books (Wales) Ltd.

AN ESTABLISHED SERIES
prepared by experienced teachers

- NOTES FOR TEACHERS AND WORKSHEETS FOR PUPILS IN ONE BOOK
- COMPREHENSIVE NATIONAL CURRICULUM COVERAGE
- THERE IS NO NEED TO BUY ADDITIONAL MATERIAL
- ALL THE MATERIAL IS PHOTOCOPIABLE
- EXCELLENT VALUE
- SAVES YOU TIME AND MONEY
- VISUALLY STIMULATING
- BOOKS SPECIFICALLY DESIGNED FOR THE KEY STAGE YOU TEACH
- FULL OF TEACHING STRATEGIES AND IDEAS
- READY-TO-USE LESSONS
- FLEXIBLE RESOURCES FOR USE BY THE WHOLE CLASS, BY GROUPS OR BY INDIVIDUAL PUPILS
- TRIED AND TESTED MATERIALS
- PHOTOCOPIABLE SHEETS TO USE AS THEY ARE OR TO REDUCE OR ENLARGE
- PHOTOCOPIABLE RECORD SHEETS FOR EACH PUPIL
- NEW TITLES PUBLISHED MONTHLY

AVAILABLE FROM
Domino Books (Wales) Ltd.,
P O Box 32, Swansea SA1 1FN.
Tel. (01792) 459378   Fax. (01792) 466337
Telephone and fax orders welcome

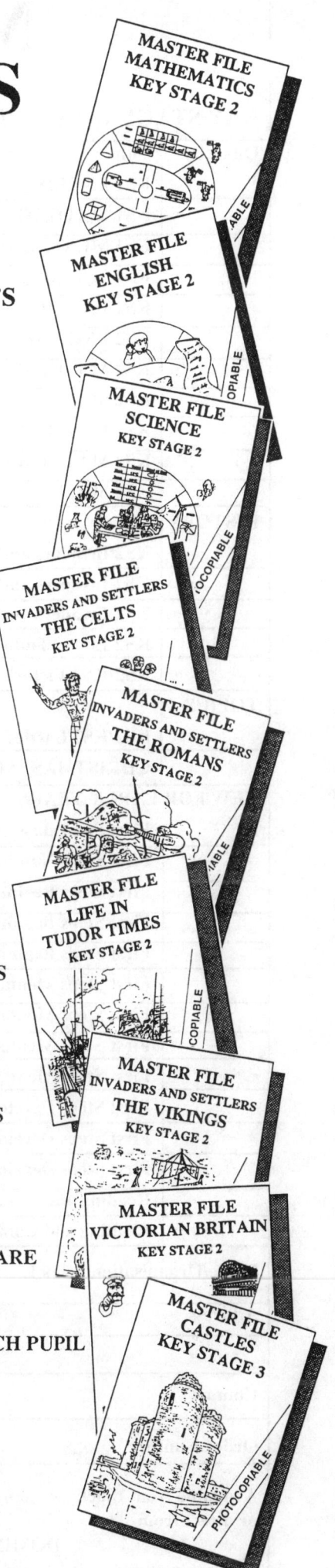

ORDER FORM OVERLEAF

MASTER FILES
ORDER FORM

KEY STAGE 1 (Age 5 - 7) KEY STAGE 2 (Age 7 - 11) KEY STAGE 3 (Age 11 - 14)

Quantity	Title	ISBN	Price	Cost
	KS1 ENGLISH	1 85772 111 X	£20.00	£
	KS1 MATHEMATICS	1 85772 107 1	£20.00	£
	KS1 MENTAL MATHEMATICS	1 85772 154 3	£20.00	£
	KS1 SCIENCE	1 85772 108 X	£20.00	£
	KS1 HISTORY	1 85772 112 8	£20.00	£
	KS2 ENGLISH	1 85772 085 7	£20.00	£
	KS2 MATHEMATICS	1 85772 086 5	£20.00	£
	KS2 SCIENCE	1 85772 087 3	£20.00	£
	KS3 ENGLISH	1 85772 127 6	£20.00	£
	KS3 MATHEMATICS	1 85772 126 8	£20.00	£
	KS3 SCIENCE	1 85772 128 4	£20.00	£
HISTORY				
	KS2 Invaders and Settlers, The Celts	1 85772 067 9	£15.95	£
	KS2 Invaders and Settlers, The Romans	1 85772 070 9	£15.95	£
	KS2 Invaders and Settlers, The Vikings	1 85772 069 5	£15.95	£
	KS2 Life in Tudor Times	1 85772 076 8	£15.95	£
	KS2/KS3 Victorian Britain	1 85772 077 6	£15.95	£
TOPICS				
	KS2/KS3 Castles	1 85772 075 X	£15.95	£
	CHRISTMAS (AGES 5 - 12)	1 85772 065 2	£20.00	£
NEW FOR EARLY YEARS				
	First Steps Basic Activities in the 3Rs	1 85772 130 6	£12.50	£
	First Steps Number and Counting	1 85772 133 0	£12.50	£
	First Steps Beginning to Read	1 85772 138 1	£12.50	£
	First Steps Beginning to Write	1 85772 139 X	£12.50	£
	First Steps Beginning Mental Maths	1 85772 142 X	£12.50	£
	First Steps Mental Maths, 5 - 6 years	1 85772 143 8	£12.50	£
	First Steps Mental Maths, 6 - 7 years	1 85772 146 2	£12.50	£
	First Steps Mental Maths, 7 - 8 years	1 85772 147 0	£12.50	£
	First Steps Mental Maths 8 - 9 years	1 85772 148 9	£12.50	£
	First Steps Developing Literacy Skills 4 - 5 years	1 85772 151 9	£12.50	£
	First Steps Developing Literacy Skills 5- 6 years	1 85772 152 7	£12.50	£
	First Steps Developing Literacy Skills 6 - 7 years	1 85772 153 5	£12.50	£
	Reading and Comprehension 5 - 7 years, Book 1	1 85772 144 6	£12.50	£
	Reading and Comprehension 5 - 7 years, Book 2	1 85772 145 4	£12.50	£
			Total	£

Name/Organisation/School

Address

Post Code   Tel.

Contact   Signature

Order Number   Date

Available from Blackwells, Foyles Bookshop, Waterstones, Welsh Books Council, WH Smith, and all good booksellers or direct from

DOMINO BOOKS (WALES) LTD, P O BOX 32, SWANSEA SA1 1FN.
Tel. 01792 459378   Fax. 01792 466337

All official orders must have an official requisition form attached (schools, educational establishments, LEAs, bookshops, libraries). Cheques with private orders please.